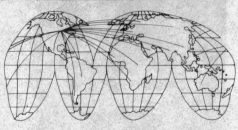

# "URBAN IRELAND"

# URBAN IRELAND

## Development
## of Towns and Villages

### CURRICULUM DEVELOPMENT UNIT

O'BRIEN

First published 1982
O'Brien Educational Ltd., 20 Victoria Road, Dublin 6.

©
Copyright reserved.

British Library Cataloguing in Publication Data
Stokes, Dermot
Urban Ireland
1. Cities and towns — Planning — Ireland
I. Title
307.7'6'09417   HT169.I/(expanded)
ISBN 0-86278-017-9 Hardback
ISBN 0-86278-018-7 Paperback

Jacket design: Conceived by O'Brien Educational and executed by Michael Furlong
Typesetting and origination: Redsetter Limited, Dublin
Printed in the Republic of Ireland by Irish Elsevier Printers, Shannon

## THE CURRICULUM DEVELOPMENT UNIT

The Curriculum Development Unit was established
in 1972. It is funded by the City of Dublin
Vocational Education Committee. It is managed
jointly by the City of Dublin Vocational Education
Committee, Trinity College, Dublin, and the
Department of Education. This book forms part of
the Humanities Curriculum.

| | |
|---|---|
| Unit Director: | Anton Trant |
| Deputy Director: | Tony Crooks |
| Humanities Team: | |
| Tony Crooks | Coordinator 1972-79 |
| Nora Godwin | 1973-79 |
| | Coordinator 1979- |
| Agnes McMahon | 1975-76 |
| Bernard O'Flaherty | 1976-78 |
| Dermot Stokes | 1977- |
| Ann Treacy | 1978-80 |

These materials have been edited for publication
by Dermot Stokes. Additional research by Michael
King.

Prior to publication, the following schools were
involved in the development, use and revision of
the collection. The suggestions and comments of
the teachers in these schools have been used as a
basis for the edition: Caritas College, Ballyfermot,
Christian Brothers School, Dun Laoghaire;
Christian Brothers School, James's Street, Coláiste
Dhulaigh, Coolock, Coláiste Éanna, Cabra; Coláiste
Eoin, Finglas; Coolmine Community School,
Clonsilla; Dun Laoghaire Community College,
Holy Child Community School, Sallynoggin;
Inchicore Vocational School; Liberties Vocational
School, Dublin; Mater Dei Secondary School, Basin
Lane; Pobal Scoil Íosa, Malahide; Rosary College,
Crumlin; Scoil Íde, Finglas; St. Dominics, Bally-
fermot; Vocational School, Ballyfermot, Vocational
School for Boys, Clogher Road, Vocational School,
Crumlin Road.

# URBAN
(adjective)
of or belonging to a city.
(From the Latin *urbanus*, an
adjective derived from *urbs*, a city.)

Page 1 - *Athlone Castle and bridge over the River Shannon.*

Page 2 - *Cork, looking towards Patrick Street. Note the numerous
Church Spires and the high ground on both sides of the city.*

Page 3 - *North Gate arch of Carrickfergus, Co. Antrim, recorded in 1914.*

Page 5 - *Georgian Dublin, number 24 Gardiner Place, March 1889.*

Above - *The Square, Kildare in 1888 with St. Brigid's ancient Cathedral, and Round Tower.*

# Contents

Introduction  8

PART 1: ANCIENT URBAN LIFE  11
Ancient Rome: Case study of a Modern City?  12

PART 2: THE DEVELOPMENT OF THE IRISH TOWN  19
Beginnings  20
Norman Towns  27
Plantation Towns  33
The Georgian Town  42
Irish Towns 1841-1980  50

PART 3: THE NEW INDUSTRIAL SOCIETY:
CASE STUDIES OF CHANGE  55
A Local World  56
Industry  57
Transport  65
Communications  75
The Urban Way of Life  80

PART 4: URBAN LIFE TODAY  83
Ireland Before the 1960s  84
After 1960: The New Urban Lifestyle  89
A Gathering Storm  94

PART 5: CITIES IN THE FUTURE  121

# Introduction

Almost one-third of the world's population lives in an urban environment. What is an 'urban environment'? Does it simply mean a place with a high population density? Or is it more than that — a certain type or quality of life?

This book will explore these questions. Urban living has existed ever since people began to live in settlements which were based on some activity other than simply the production of enough food for its inhabitants. Trade, manufacturing and, later, mechanised industry have all caused urban development. Cities of ancient civilisations, with structures and problems not unlike those in our cities today, have disappeared. New planned cities have grown from nothing.

There were some eras in the history of Ireland which saw particular urban growth. This book will trace the development of Irish towns and show how the city had different meanings and functions in these different eras — a place for trading, an expression of the height of civilisation, a hope of employment for refugees from a poverty-stricken countryside, a leader in fashion and sophistication, an industrial, commercial and administrative centre.

In present times, urban living is no longer confined to the city streets. It has become a uniform mass-produced lifestyle throughout the country, raising the general standards of housing, transport and communications, and also killing individuality and tradition.

Life in cities today raises many issues: everyone needs housing, flexible transport systems, consumer goods, but at what price? What is causing so much disaffection on the part of city-dwellers? Can they adapt quickly enough to the constant change around them? Is change itself the only thing one can be really sure of?

If the present growth rate of our cities continues, decisions will have to be made. Many of these decisions will be about how land should be used — for housing, amenities, roads or industry? With new technological developments, we may possibly conduct all aspects of our lives in one place — work, home life, leisure — making the bustling, noisy, traffic-choked city street obsolete. Maybe the present problems in our cities will finally destroy the very environment which caused them. The final section of the book looks at the city in the future, and at the future of the city.

# THE LARGE CITIES OF THE WORLD

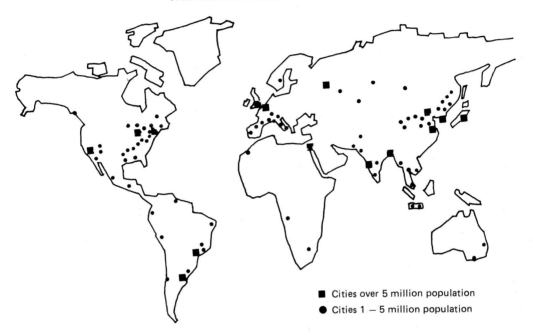

■ Cities over 5 million population
● Cities 1 — 5 million population

## PROPORTION OF WORLD POPULATION LIVING IN URBAN AREAS

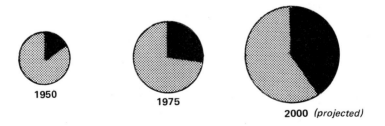

1950

1975

2000 *(projected)*

Black = Urban population

## AN EAR'S EYEFUL

Well . . .
In the morning it's got singing birds,
Magpies, robins, sparrows, crows,
Until the waking hum of the sleeping giant
Drowns them out,
It's got the beeps and barps and roars
Of cars and trucks and cranes,
The signs and sounds of Men At Work,
*Lower down, lower down, that's it.*
*O.K. Tommy, take her out,*
*Willie, put on the tea,*
*You! Gerrowa the bleedin' way!*

The hummmm of diesel, the hisssss of steam,
The clank of caterpillar tracks,
Beer barrels bounce on a boozer's beaut,
Machinegun street-drills crash.
And then there's the factories, the bakeries,
    the shops,
The cafes, the waterfalls, the cops,
Street singers, humdingers, and gunslingers,
Steeltips on the streets, clogs on the paths,
The clicking of doors and the clanging
    of windows,
The swishing of blinds, the humming of lifts,
The ringing of cash registers,
And the people, moving talking,
Whistling, laughing, until the dimmer
    hours . . .

*Gerrup there Charlie, ah the hard Paddy,*
*Evenin' Herrallurpress,*
*Giss a few pence an' I'll say a prayer,*
*Move along now miss, and don't cause a fuss.*

Sales, bargains, throbbing feet,
My corns have paid their dues,
*"How much are them jeeyans there,*
*How much for the shewez?*
*Are ya jokin'! No thanks Molly!*
*Ya can keep that pair for oul' George Colley.*

*TEN PENCE EACH THE BANANNITS!*
*TWENTY PEE THE SALADS!*
*Do you want the orange love?*
*GET YAR GRAPEFRUWETS!*
*LUVVLY JOOCY MELLANS!*
*FISH, ordnges, FISH, ordnges,"*
*(Cockerels, quarehawks and fruit,*
*Molly Mellon alive alive-O')*

In other quarters they dress in twill,
And handmade leather boots,
And talk of Business and Finance,
Of horses and women . . .
And they smoke cheroots.

*Dermot Stokes*

*Part One*

ANCIENT URBAN LIFE

# Ancient Rome:
## Case Study of a Modern City?

Rome was not the first great city. Others had flourished before its time. However, since the word *urban* comes from a Roman word, perhaps a look at that city, and what its citizens meant when they used the word *urbs,* will identify some of the characteristics of urban life. As we shall see, there is far more in common between the lifestyle of this ancient city and our present-day lifestyle than one might think.

Almost 3000 years ago the first people settled on the plain of Latium in the centre of Italy. They built their mud and wattle huts close to the only place on the plain where the River Tiber is shallow enough for travellers to cross it. The site also had the advantage of being close to several hills, which gave it natural protection. From this beginning, Rome grew into a walled town; it became a trade centre, for Latium and then for Italy and, finally, for the entire Mediterranean.

By the 1st century AD Rome was the centre of an empire which stretched from Germany in the north, to Egypt in the south, from Spain in the west, and to Asia in the east. This empire was administered by a civil service centred on Rome and controlled by an army. Grain ships from Egypt and boats laden with olive oil and wine from Greece and Africa arrived daily and discharged their loads into the warehouses at Ostia, a seaport of Rome.

As Rome became more wealthy as the trading and administrative centre of an empire, more and more people came to live there. By the 1st century AD the population had increased to over one million people.

Rome had come a long way from the rough and ready settlement it once was. Emperors vied with each other to build paved streets and stone and marble public buildings which would make the city more beautiful.

### HOUSING CONDITIONS

Emperors might have given Rome an appearance worthy of the capital of a great empire, but they did little to make life comfortable for the poor. Most of the people in Rome lived in large tenement blocks called *insulae*. Most of these 'high-rise' blocks were four or five storeys high and con-

### THE 14 DISTRICTS OF ROME
### A SURVEY

| | | |
|---|---|---|
| 28 libraries | 6 obelisks | 8 bridges |
| 8 parks | 11 fora | 10 basilicas |
| 11 public baths | 19 aquaducts | 29 chief roads |
| 2 circuses | 2 amphitheatres | 2 market places |
| 3 theatres | 4 training schools | 212 statues |
| 37 city gates | 46,602 apartment houses | 1,790 private houses |
| 290 warehouses | 856 baths | 1,352 fountains |
| 254 cornmills | 46 brothels | 144 public lavatories |

*Source: Survey commissioned by the Emperor Constantine in the 4th century AD.*

tained many small uncomfortable rooms. Often, the ground floor was divided into shops, which opened straight out onto the street, and the dwellings, one family per room, were on the higher storeys. Access was nearly always by a wooden ladder, and lighting came from one large window. In this room the family cooked, ate and slept.

There was no plumbing in the upper storeys; most people had to fill their jugs at the corner fountain, and slops and garbage were tossed into the streets from the window in the hope that the next fall of rain would wash them into the sewers. No heating and bad insulation made the upper rooms very hot in the summer and cold in winter.

These buildings were downright dangerous. The Emperor Augustus forbade the construction of *insulae* over 21 metres high, because of the poor quality of their construction.

'Much of this city is supported by props', Juvenal, a Roman poet, wrote at the time, 'In this way the bailiff stops the houses from collapsing. After he has plastered over the gaping hole of an old crack, he expects you to sleep securely. And if there happens to be a fire, you have no chance at all. Often the blaze can have spread from the ground floor upwards as far as the third storey before anybody living above knows anything about it, and the very last person to know is the person living up in the attic' (*Satires*).

Life was very different for rich Romans. Their spacious mansions, usually built around a shady courtyard with a fountain, had marble columns, walls and floors. The interiors were hung with opulent curtains and furnished with ivory, bronze and rare woods. Artists were paid to decorate their villas, with frescoes on the walls and mosaics on the floors.

*Tenement dwellings or insulae in Ancient Rome.*

### THE CITY STREETS

The Romans boasted of having 112 kilometres of streets in their city. Most of these were narrow and congested. During the day, everything took place out in the street — buying and selling, haggling and shouting in open-air markets; craftsmen in make-shift workshops; beggars crying out to passers-by; even schoolmasters and their pupils, voices raised to be heard over the general racket.

There was so much noise and congestion on the streets that Caesar passed a degree which banned all traffic from the streets of Rome during the hours of daylight. However, when darkness fell, peace did not come with it. Juvenal says that the night traffic and noise condemned all Romans to everlasting insomnia. 'What sleep is possible in a lodging?' he asks, 'The crossing of wagons in the narrow, winding streets,

*Buying and selling in a Roman street-market (from a stone relief, 2 A.D.).*

the swearing of drivers brought to a standstill, would snatch sleep from the Emperor Claudius himself.'

14

## WATER SUPPLY

The *Cloaca Maxima,* the main artery of Rome's system of sewers, can still be seen today. Its semicircular arch, five metres in diameter, was built 2,500 years ago and still functions, emptying sewage into the River Tiber.

According to Constantine's survey, 19 aquaducts led to Rome, carrying water into the city. The Aqua Claudia was 70 kilometres long; water ran from the hills through underground channels and then through pipes on top of large arches into the city. The construction of these aquaducts was a considerable technical feat and employed many workmen. However, despite this water supply to the city, it was rare for the tenement dwellers to have more than one water pipe at the bottom of their tenement.

## WORK

Wealthy Romans were merchants, landowners, politicians and imperial officers. They dressed in expensive clothes, and used perfumes, cosmetics and jewellery. Their diet was far more varied than that of the ordinary citizens. Meat, fish and fowl were plentiful, as were a wide variety of fruits and vegetables. At a dinner they might eat up to seven courses. Their children went to schools where they were usually taught by Greeks, whose civilisation was much admired by the Romans.

The work which supported this opulence was carried on by lesser civil servants, lawyers, shopkeepers, craftsmen and slaves. Country estates owned by the wealthy were maintained by a large number of staff, including clothmakers, potters and winemakers, as well as cooks, cleaners and labourers. Many Romans worked on the docks, or in the warehouses beside them; others maintained the many public buildings and monuments, and most of the rest were artisans and retailers — greengrocers, market gardeners, fishermen, tavern keepers, goldsmiths, jewellers, shoemakers, ropemakers, furriers, carpenters, metalworkers. Most of these people lived in the tenements. Their diet consisted largely of wheat flour made into bread and porridge, flavoured with herbs and spices, and eaten with vegetables.

## URBAN UNREST

Not everyone had work. Thousands of people, pouring into the capital from the countryside, meant that there were always more in the city than jobs to do. The number of people living in poverty was high. The poor were given 'doles' of free corn; up to one-third of the city's population received this kind of aid.

Street riots, petty crime and drunkenness were some of the ways in which Rome's poor frequently expressed its anger and frustration. They were a real headache to the municipal authorities; Juvenal also had his bit to say about them. Here he encounters an angry drunk:

'He stands facing you and orders you to stop; you must obey, for what else can you do when a madman forces you, especially if he is stronger than you are? . . . It is all the same whether you try to say anything or remain silent, you are going to get beaten up in any case . . . After you've been thrashed with fisticuffs, you have no choice but to beg to be allowed to retire from the scene with the few teeth left to you.'                    *Satires*

Unrest of this nature became rarer after the Emperor Augustus formed an organised police-force. Three cohorts, each one thousand in size, operated in a military fashion and kept the Roman mob under strict control. If things got bad, they could call in auxiliary troops to give them more weight.

Augustus also believed that the poor could be distracted from their grievances. He increased the number of public entertainments, to which everyone had access, in the hope of keeping the people amused.

### LEISURE AND ENTERTAINMENT

One of the more regular pleasures in life for the citizens of Rome was a visit to the public baths. These were something like the health and leisure centres of today, housing shops, gardens, gymnasia, massage rooms and even libraries and museums, as well as a variety of different hot and cold baths.

### AT THE BATHS

'I live over a bathing establishment.

Picture to yourself now the assortment of voices, the sound of which is enough to sicken one. When the stronger fellows are exercising and swinging heavy leaden weights in their hands, when they are working hard or pretending to be working hard, I hear their groans; and whenever they release their pent-up breath, I hear their hissing and jarring breathing. When I have to do with a lazy fellow who is content with a cheap rubdown, I hear the slap of the hand pummeling his shoulders, changing its sound according as the hand is laid on flat or curved. If now a professional ball player comes along and begins to keep score, I am done for. Add to this the arrest of a brawler or a thief, and the fellow who always likes to hear his own voice in the bath, and those who jump into the pool with a mighty splash as they strike the water. In addition to those whose voices are, if nothing else, natural, imagine the hair plucker keeping up a constant chatter in his thin and strident voice, to attract more attention, and never silent except when he is plucking armpits and making the customer yell instead of yelling himself. It disgusts me to enumerate the varied cries of the sausage dealer and confectioner and of all the peddlers of the cook shops, hawking their wares, each with his own peculiar intonation.'

*Seneca: 'Moral Epistles'*

Typical urban dwellers, the Romans loved spectator sports and chariot racing was among the more popular. The *Circus Maximus,* which could hold up to 300,000 spectators — almost one-third of the population of Rome — was the largest chariot-racing track. The track cover was 550 metres long and 18 metres wide. There were four racing stables, the Reds, Whites, the Greens, and the Blues; each maintained its own training school for

*The Circus Maximus which could hold up to 300,000 spectators.*

drivers and bred its own horses. All four teams usually took part in a race, and the spectators gambled heavily on the outcome. The most successful of the charioteers were considered superstars. Chariot racing was a dangerous sport, the chariots were very light and could easily overturn, and while the best charioteers could count up to 1,000 wins, others died after only a few races.

The Romans also loved to attend the amphitheatres, the most famous of which was the Colosseum. This theatre could hold 50,000 spectators who could all reach their own numbered seat by entering through separate levels and walking down wide passages. It was also possible to empty the amphitheatre within a few minutes. Every now and then, the arena would be flooded for naval displays, but the two main types of entertainment in the amphitheatre were gladiatorial shows and animal hunts.

### A GLADIATORIAL EVENT

'I chanced to stop in at a midday show, expecting fun, wit, and some relaxation, when men's eyes take respite from the slaughter of their fellow men. It was just the reverse. The preceding combats were merciful by comparison; now all trifling is put aside and it is pure murder. The men have no protective covering. Their entire bodies are exposed to the blows, and no blow is ever struck in vain . . . . In the morning men are thrown to the lions and the bears, at noon they are thrown to the spectators. The spectators call for the slayer to be thrown to those who in turn will slay him, and they detain the victor for another butchering. The outcome for the combatants is death; the fight is waged with sword and fire. This goes on while the arena is free. 'But one of them was a highway robber, he killed a man!' Because he killed he deserved to suffer this punishment, granted . . . . 'Kill him! Lash him! Burn him! Why does he meet the sword so timidly? Why doesn't he kill boldly? Why doesn't he die game? Whip him to meet his wounds! Let them trade blow for blow, chests bare and within reach!' And when the show stops for intermission, 'Let's have men killed mean-

*Roman Superstar: This charioteer was one of the idols of the crowd at the Circus Maximus.*

while! Let's not have nothing going on!' '    *Seneca: Moral Epistles*

### THE END OF ANCIENT ROME

The Roman Empire lasted for over 1,000 years. Towards the end of that time barbarian tribes began to invade the provinces of the empire, and by the 5th century AD they had arrived at Rome itself. In quick succession, the city was sacked by the Goths and the Vandals and, finally, the emperor was deposed.

As the empire collapsed, life in Rome continued much as before, although with each passing year taxes became heavier, to maintain the army and to pay barbarians not to attack the borders. Inflation rose and the economy ground to a halt. Plague and famine increased the problems. In the end the empire was unable to defend itself, and the city ceased to function as a city.

Rome did not disappear. Without the strength and riches of the empire behind it, it went into decline. The population dropped as people no longer could make a living there; elaborate baths, circuses and amphitheatres were no longer needed; buildings and streets fell into disrepair. The same fate befell other great cities in the world, in Asia, in the regions now known as the Middle East, in Africa, in South and Central America. In some cases they fell to invaders or disease. In others the cause of their downfall is unknown.

Present-day transport, industry, communications and information technology make our lifestyle very different from that of Rome 2,000 years ago. At the same time we have much in common with the Romans, from spectator sports and huge building projects to problems such as unrest, bad housing and economic problems. An ancient Roman might well be baffled by the operations of a computer or a television, but a family living in sub-standard housing in Rome might feel much the same way as a family living in an overcrowded flat in Dublin today; the anger and frustration of a rioter in the streets of ancient Rome would not have been much different from those of a rioter in present-day Liverpool and London, and wouldn't a crowd spilling out of the Colosseum after an exciting day's games feel much the same as a crowd spilling out of Wembley Stadium or Croke Park?

Rome was once rich and self-confident, the most advanced and civilised city of its day. Could a similar fate befall the rich and sophisticated cities of today? Terrible warfare and disease are still possible, more so now than ever before. Perhaps our grasp on the urban lifestyle we have embraced is not as firm as we would like to think.

*Part Two*

# THE DEVELOPMENT OF
# THE IRISH TOWN

# Beginnings

As the Roman Empire collapsed, Celtic Ireland was a land of forests and fields. It had kings, warriors and poets, but most of its people were farmers living in small isolated settlements. These were usually in the fortified ring-forts known as raths. Most of these only contained a single farmstead, but larger and stronger raths have been found which probably belonged to kings and nobles.

CELTIC IRELAND

*Here's my story; the stag cries,*
*Winter snarls as summer dies.*

*The wind bullies the low sun*
*in poor light; the seas moan.*

*Shapeless bracken is turning red,*
*The wildgoose raises its desperate head.*

*Birds' wings where fields are hoary.*
*The world is ice. That's my story.*

Anonymous 7th-13th century
*(translated by Brendan Kennelly)*

Other structures in Celtic Ireland were hill-forts. They were larger and had more uses than the raths. Some hill-forts were not only places of defence, but were also the sites of assemblies and religious ceremonies. These included the legendary Tara and Emain Macha. Other less important sites were centres of activities for the inhabitants of the smaller kingdoms known as *tuatha*.

The larger royal sites were occupied for thousands of years, some from the late Stone Age onwards and some of them were probably quite large settlements by the time Christianity came to Ireland. While they would have had some of the things we look for in a town — they were continuously occupied collections of permanent buildings — they were not towns.

MONASTIC SETTLEMENTS

The arrival of Christianity brought a new form of settlement to Ireland. By

**HILL-FORTS**

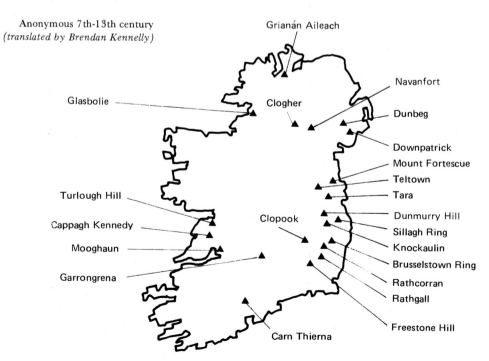

Grianán Aileach
Navanfort
Glasbolie
Clogher
Dunbeg
Downpatrick
Mount Fortescue
Teltown
Tara
Turlough Hill
Clopook
Dunmurry Hill
Cappagh Kennedy
Sillagh Ring
Mooghaun
Knockaulin
Brusselstown Ring
Garrongrena
Rathcorran
Rathgall
Freestone Hill
Carn Thierna

*An early Christian Monastic Settlement — Innishmurray Island off the coast of Sligo. This is built inside an earlier pre-historic stone cashel.*

*Clonmacnoise Monastery dating from early Christian Ireland. Built on a hill it overlooks the surrounding countryside.*

In 795 AD the monastery on Lambay Island was raided by Vikings in search of gold and silverware, food, corn and armour and slaves. At first the raids were hit and run affairs, but from around 840 the Vikings began to winter in Ireland, building stockades around their camps to protect their ships and plunder.

They chose sites by river estuaries, for fresh water and sheltered anchorage. Very often the river was forded nearby, and roads led inland. These stockades were built all around the coasts. In many cases they did not prosper as settlements, but some of them were well placed to control trade between Ireland, Britain and Europe. As the Vikings moved towards trading and away from plunder, they built harbours for the larger vessels they began to use. Among the locations of these harbours were Dublin, Waterford, Wexford, Cork, Youghal and Limerick. On these sites the first 'towns' in Ireland began to develop.

For a long time these towns were not very different from the

the 8th century there were several hundred monasteries throughout the country. Apart from the monks themselves, the larger monasteries also had students, lay farmers and craftworkers. In time, the dependents and clients of the monasteries probably built huts outside the walls, especially after they became centres for metalworking and other crafts.

The larger monasteries were usually built within a circular enclosure, like a rath. The buildings consisted of a church or churches, the monks' cells, the library and scriptorium or copying room, the refectory and workshop. The farm buildings were outside the walls. It is not easy to know how many people lived in the Celtic monasteries, but few can have had anything like 1,000 people. The very largest, however, were in many ways close to being towns. The monks built the first tall buildings in Ireland. Their famous Round Towers have not been imitated by any other builders.

**VIKING PORTS**

monasteries and hill-forts, in appearance at least. The houses were made of post-and-wattle, and thatched with straw. The streets were narrow and often muddy. In many cases, such as Dublin, the 'towns' were even on or beside monastic settlements. Many of the jobs being carried out were also to be found in settlements all over the country.

The most important difference between the Viking towns and the settlements in Celtic Ireland was that the Viking towns were built on sites that were well situated for trade, by people who were fine sailors and merchants. Elsewhere in Ireland, people lived in small, self-sufficient communities, producing what they needed for themselves and perhaps exchanging the surplus for some other goods. The lifestyle of the townspeople was that of craftsmen and traders, based on handling, re-shaping, buying and selling the produce drawn from elsewhere, and on supervising and taxing the passage of goods in and out of their settlement. The towns were able to support a large population, most of whom saw their town as a permanent home.

*Part of the old Viking/Medieval town of Dublin seen during the excavations at Wood Quay during the 1970s. Now two tower blocks — The Civic Offices occupy this site.*

## The Shape of Irish Towns

Ireland's 'settlement pattern' is varied. It ranges from isolated country houses, west coast 'ribbon development', to large towns and cities. The two main influences on the location of Irish towns have been communications and defence. The Irish town was a market and service centre for the people of an area. Travel by horse and foot determined the location and distance between centres. As a result, there is a pattern which is found throughout the country.

Smaller settlements are from 6 to 12 kilometres apart, a few hours' walking distance. The larger centres are from 25 to 50 kilometres apart, and the larger regional centres of 10,000 people and upwards, are 95 kilometres apart. The settlements themselves fall into the following categories:

*The Crossroads Villages:* A simple settlement, with a small group of houses and one or two shops. The *clachan* is a variant — it is a cluster of farm buildings, found in the West, south Leinster and the Mourne country.

**COLLINSTOWN CO. WESTMEATH**

*Market Towns:* This is the commonest type of settlement in Ireland, North and South. Its population can range from 500 to 50,000. Market towns are complex economic units, with a wide range of shops, and housing.

BAILIEBORO CO. CAVAN

*Tralee, Co. Kerry, during the Rose of Tralee Festival. This town was founded by the Normans.*

*Resorts:* Developed in the 19th century with growing popularity of holidays, aided by railways in particular. Usually on the coast, though some are inland, like Killarney and Lisdoonvarna.

*The Agricultural Village:* Acts as a local centre. There are a few shops, with a church, a school, and perhaps a hall. The rest is housing, usually one or two storeys.

*Estate villages* are variations, and have been built by local landlords.

*Fishing Port:* Ireland's coast is dotted with fishing ports of many sizes, from small villages to large towns like Killybegs, Kilkeel and Dunmore East. Fishing is also an important industry in other ports, such as Galway, Kinsale, Dun Laoghaire and Howth.

DUNMORE EAST CO. WATERFORD

*Transport Towns:* These are towns which expanded after the development of railways and canals, e.g. Dundalk, Portadown, Newry, Cobh and Tullamore.

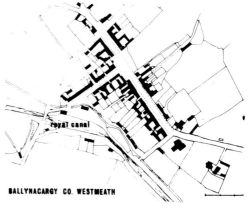

BALLYNACARGY CO. WESTMEATH

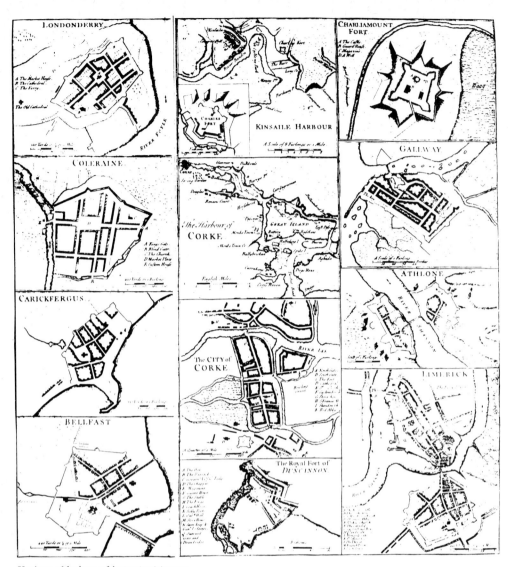

*Various old plans of important towns.*

*Industrial Towns:* Shopping and services are not limited in industrial towns where the emphasis is on industry and housing. Portlaw, Clara and Kilbeggan are in the south of Ireland, and there are many examples in the North.

*Commuter Towns:* Small towns that are expanding very rapidly due to closeness to major developing centre. Swords, Co. Dublin, is a good example, as is Oranmore, Co. Galway. Often these towns have the centre of an agricultural village or market town and are surrounded by suburban housing.

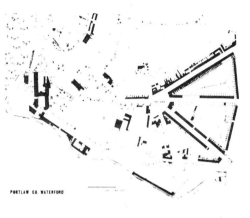

PORTLAW CO. WATERFORD

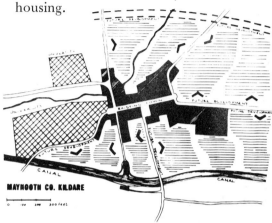

MAYNOOTH CO. KILDARE

0    100   200   300 feet

# Norman Towns

In May 1169 a small force of Anglo-Norman soldiers, led by Robert Fitz Stephen, landed at Bannow Bay, Co. Wexford. It was the first step in an attempt at conquering Ireland. The Normans were the most successful soldiers of their day, and soon controlled large tracts of Ireland. Among their first strongholds were the Viking ports of Wexford, Waterford and Dublin, which they captured with much bloodshed.

After the first military victories of the Normans came the settlers and a century of new town building. In 1175 the Treaty of Mellifont was signed between their king, Henry II of England, and Rory O'Connor, the most powerful Irish king. It signed over all of the present province of Leinster, and part of Waterford, to the Normans. Soon afterward,

however, the Normans moved beyond these borders. By 1220 they had conquered most of the country, except for south and west Ulster.

Once the Normans had conquered a district, large areas of land were granted by the king to a principal tenant who let smaller areas to sub-tenants. They, in turn, let their lands to others. The next stage was the building of forts or strongholds to maintain control over the lands. At this point settlers began to arrive, and settlements grew around the castles and churches. Most of these were never to become more than villages, but some received permission to hold markets and fairs, which increased their importance. These settlements were most numerous in the east and south of Ireland. Many areas, such as the central plain and the highland areas of Wicklow, south-west Munster, Connacht and Ulster, saw little town-building.

The Normans chose the sites for their settlements with care. Many were situated on old monastic sites, markets or meeting places. Very often the most successful settlements developed around the manors of the most powerful lords.

Perhaps the major advantage these settlements had over others was a favourable location. When the Normans over-ran Ireland the first conquerors had the choice of the best sites. These were usually in places that were easy to defend, and were often on or near river-crossings on the larger rivers. At that time Ireland was densely forested and many of its rivers could carry boats much further inland than they can today. When the Normans controlled the river-crossings, they also controlled the movement of people and freight. Such a location also benefited the towns when it came to trade. Most of the towns and villages held markets and fairs, but any goods that were to travel any distance, especially exports, had to go through a town on a major road or river.

From this it follows that the most important towns in Norman Ireland were the ports, which linked this island with Britain and Europe. The ports of the south coast, New Ross, Waterford, Youghal and Cork, handled over 70 per cent of trade in Norman Ireland, and those of the east coast, Drogheda, Dublin and Wexford,

## IRISH TOWNS FOUNDED BY THE NORMANS

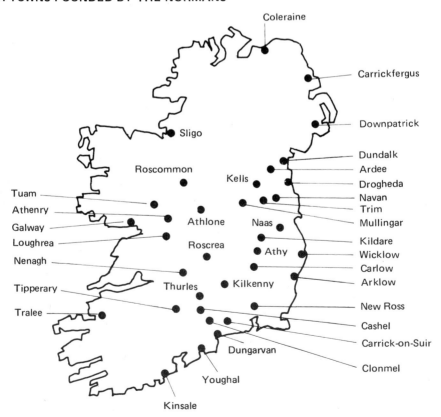

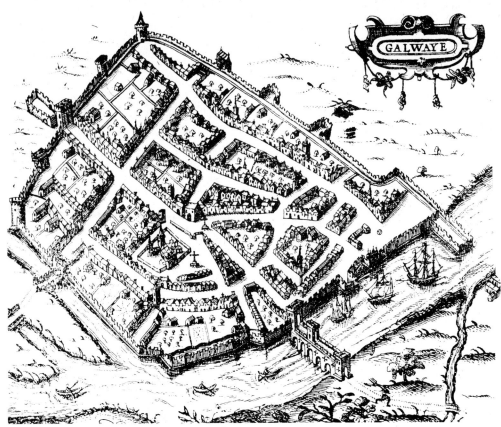

*The walled City of Galway in 1610, from Speede's map.*

handled 25 per cent. The remaining 5 per cent was divided between the west and north. The principal exports were fish, hides and skins and linen. Imports included cloth, salt, wine and foodstuffs.

### MEDIEVAL TOWN LIFE

The narrow alleyways that twisted and turned between the buildings of the old towns led to the different quarters, in which various parts of the town's work were carried on. Craftsmen worked outdoors when possible, for the sake of good light. People working at the same craft often gathered in one street.

A town brought together people who lived different lives and who were in town for different purposes. Large numbers of the inhabitants of Norman Irish towns were immigrants from England and Europe. Some of the towns had Irish quarters, and most of the ports also had Viking suburbs. The market place was a meeting place where being a stranger was nothing strange. In the countryside, centuries of experience gave every activity its proper place, but in the crowded disorder of a growing town, new ideas and new ways of doing things were more readily accepted.

There had to be regulations and planning, supervision of trade and manufacture, and taxes had to be raised to pay for the government, defence and development of the town. Where many families were crowded so close together, problems arose. Fire spread rapidly between the thatched, woodframed houses. Disease could spread almost as quickly, especially if the water supply was contaminated. Unpaved streets

*Life in a medieval Irish town as depicted by 'Holinshed' in his Chronicles published in 1577.*

*A battle scene during the campaign of Hugh O'Neill in the 16th century as depicted by 'Holinshed'.*

became a sea of mud in wet weather. The town air was fouled by piles of household waste, in which pigs rooted ceaselessly. Pits had to be dug outside the town for toilet waste. Bridges, quays and warehouses had to be constructed and maintained. Perhaps most important, the town had to be protected.

The townspeople built walls and checked everyone who came and went. The gates were locked against all intruders at night. Small towns were protected by large ditches topped by wooden palisades, but larger towns had walls of stone. The old seal of the City of Dublin shows one of the towered gates in the city walls. The walls gave the townspeople a sense of security. In the rest of Norman Ireland, the powerful lords who owned vast estates of land, also owned the lives of the people who lived there. Many of the lords had their own armies to protect their interests. The townspeople, on the other hand, were free. The walls of their town were as much a way of showing this independence as actual protection from any landowning baron.

The other threat that existed came from the Gaelic tribes living in the surrounding countryside. Townspeople lived in constant fear of attack and went to great lengths to protect themselves. From 1315 to 1318 an army, led by Edward Bruce, the King of Scotland's brother, fought a fierce campaign against the Normans of Ireland and came close to Dublin in 1317. In desperation, its people tore down the bridge over the Liffey to isolate the city and repair its walls.

This violent society was also religious. Wealthy rulers gave lands for the building of monasteries so that the monks would pray for their souls. Many towns were surrounded by monastic buildings. However, the only buildings of the medieval era to equal its castles and forts in magnitude, were its cathedrals. Just outside Dublin, the Normans built St. Patrick's Cathedral in a marsh by a holy well, below the little wooden houses of the town.

It is difficult to say which towns were the most important in the years between 1300 and 1500, as many vital facts, such as population numbers, are no longer available. However, from what is known it seems that Dublin, the seat of government, was the largest and most important, followed by New Ross, the largest port. Kilkenny was probably the biggest inland town.

Norman town-building reached its peak around the year 1250, and soon afterwards the Gaelic Irish began to win back territory. The colony began to weaken and trade fell. Many settlements were over-run and deserted. Even a large and successful town like Wexford declined. The Bruce invasion of 1315-18 caused much damage. In 1348 the terrible outbreak of disease throughout Europe known as 'The Black Death' killed many town-dwellers. For the next century and a half town life was in decline in Ireland, with only the larger and better fortified towns surviving in Irish-held lands.

The jurors say that William and Nicholas Beaghan made an affray and bloodshed on Shane Morgho. They are fined 7/6 Irish.

Also that Alison White, wife of John Hoyle, made affray, assault and bloodshed on Margaret Beaghan, wife of James Rowgan. She is fined 20d.

Also that Patrick Browne made assault and bloodshed on Margaret Beaghan. He is fined for a similar offence on Geoffrey Beaghan, but he is let off the fine until the next court.

Also the jurors present John Hoyle because his pigs spoiled the commons belonging to this manor. Ordered that he correct and amend (that is, harrow and smooth the same) before the 25th of next month, otherwise to forfeit 6/8 Irish.

Also they present Nicholas Clody for stopping a certain watercourse running in the southern part of this town. He is given until the 24th of next month to remove the said nuisance.

As no sale had been made of the swarm of bees found as strays in the last court, it is ordered that they shall be sold.

*Court of Our Lady the Queen, held before Gerald Dillon, Friday 15th February 1593*

* * *

The jurors say that John Hoyle did not smooth and harrow the common which his pigs destroyed on the 25th February last, according to the order made in the last court. He was fined.

They present William Pursell, John Hales, and John Talbot for keeping she-goats against the rule, to the annoyance of the inhabitants. Therefore each shall make amends as ordered.

The jurors present James Bombes for assault on Margaret Beaghan. Fined 20d. *Great Court of Our Lady Queen Elizabeth, held before Gerald Dillon, April 30th, 1593*

* * *

It is ordered by the consent of the homagers that between this and 1st August next every cottier shall find one man, and every farmer and freeholder shall find two men, to clean a ditch in the town. The constables and John Hales and Richard Burghill and appointed to settle the day for cleaning. And anyone not obeying this order shall forfeit 6d sterling, to be spent by the said constables and assistants to supply the absence of labour. *Great Court held Friday June 21st 1594*

* * *

It is ordered, by common consent, that every inhabitant within the manor shall find one person with the necessary tools to purge a certain pool now in the town of Crumlin, to the great nuisance of the inhabitants, and other her majesties subjects, two days between this and Michaelmas next by the direction of the constable. Whosoever defaults shall forfeit 6s. 8d. *Court held before Edward Johnson, Friday 8th April 1597*

# Plantation Towns

In 1485 Henry Tudor became Henry VII of England after the Battle of Bosworth ended the Wars of the Roses. He spent the rest of his life restoring order in England. It was not until his son Henry VIII came to the throne in 1509 that an English king was able to turn his attention to the state of the colony of Ireland.

Over 200 years of warfare had reduced the loyal area of Ireland to a small strip around Dublin known as the Pale. Elsewhere, many of the settlements established by the Normans had been over-run by the Gaelic Irish and had virtually ceased to exist. Sligo, it seems, was the only Norman town to continue its existence under the control of a Gaelic lord. Cavan and Longford were the only examples of actual town development in a Gaelic lordship.

Kilkenny was the largest inland town. It was located on the banks of the Nore, which linked it with other trade centres to the north and south, and it was in one of the most important areas of Norman settlement. It developed into a major centre of trade and manufacture. Its 'Common Book', written between 1352 and 1537, lists many occupations: labourers, bakers, tailors, shoemakers, fullers, ale-wives, brewers, merchants, fishermen, cordwainers, dyers, glove-makers, tanners, carpenters, weavers, masons, butchers, cooks, clerks and officials. Laws were passed to govern the jobs carried out by these trades, and control of the town was in the hands of a small number of merchant families. It was

*The River Lee and Quays, Cork city, an important port of the south coast.*

also an important military and religious centre.

Kilkenny was unlike most other inland towns. Under the protection of the very powerful Earls of Ormonde (the Butler family) it did not suffer as much from the attacks of the Gaelic Irish as other towns. Other towns to survive to 1508 in the most heavily colonised area were small walled towns such as Navan, Mullingar and Naas, and inland ports such as Athlone. There were few other towns inland, except for religious centres like Armagh. Port towns, on the whole, survived, although warfare, disease and the activities of pirates reduced their prosperity. The most important ports were still those on the south coast, especially Cork, Limerick and Waterford.

*Carrickfergus, from a 16th century drawing. A wooden structure in the harbour is being filled with rocks to form a pier. Note also the beehive huts of the Gaelic Irish.*

## PLANTATIONS

Until 1541 kings of England were known as 'Lord of Ireland'. In that year, however, Henry VIII was declared 'King of Ireland' by the Irish parliament in Dublin. It was the beginning of a new era. Like all rulers of England since then, Henry wanted Ireland to be peaceful and friendly. Otherwise it could be used to destabilise England by its enemies.

Henry worked mostly by persuasion, getting the Irish lords to surrender their lands to him, then re-granting them back to them. Once the Irish had gone through this procedure, their lands could be confiscated if they rebelled. Once the lands were confiscated, new settlers could be brought in.

---

### IRISH PORTS 1509

Galway: one of the most isolated and independent towns in Ireland. It was a major port. Its merchant families (the tribes of Galway) promoted trade with Britain, France, Portugal and Andalusia, as well as with the Gaelic Irish of Connacht, Clare Island and the Aran Islands. One of its main imports was wine. It exported fish, hides, leather, wool, grain, timber.

Limerick was large and well populated, on an ideal location on the Shannon estuary. A major port, it traded with France and especially Spain and Portugal. These were important salmon fisheries on the Shannon. It was one of the best fortified Irish towns.

Baltimore,[1] Tralee[2] and Dingle,[3] three small ports, principally important for fishing.

Kinsale: a major fishing port for Irish and foreign fishermen. Also traded with south-west Britain, France and Spain.

Sligo: a Norman town under Gaelic control. It was originally a military and religious centre, but had developed as a port, exporting herrings in particular.

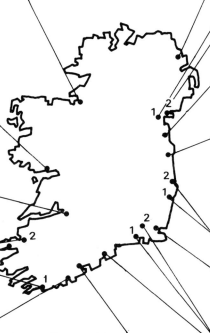

Cork: a small but wealthy port, described as "the fourth city of Ireland".
It had a fine harbour and strong trade links with south-west England, Flanders, France and Spain.

Youghal: a small port. Imported wine, salt, manufactured goods and iron. Exported salmon, cloth, timber.

Carrickfergus, once the most important Norman town in Ulster, was not a port of any great importance in 1508.

Dundalk[1] and Carlingford[2] were small ports.

Drogheda was not as large as Dublin, but carried on trade with Liverpool and Chester that was almost as valuable as Dublin's.

Dublin: centre of government, law, justice, manufacturing, religion, services and trade. Served a very large area of Leinster. Also served as exporting port for parts of Ulster with which it was linked by sea. Carried on an extensive trade with Chester and Liverpool.

Arklow[1] and Wicklow[2]: small ports.

Wexford: a major fishing port and timber exporter.

Waterford:[1] the second largest and second wealthiest town in Ireland. A very important port. Rivers Nore, Barrow and Suir connected it with a huge inland area. Waterford was a major fishing port, and had a huge volume of exports and imports to and from Britain and Europe. New Ross[2] had declined in wealth and importance over the previous 200 years.

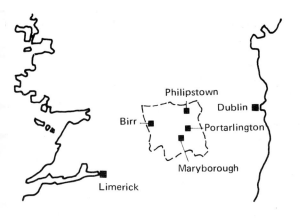

The first plantation was in the counties of Leix and Offaly, on the borders of the Pale. Some of the Irish were expelled from the area and settlers were introduced from the early 1560s. Two towns were built around the forts of Maryborough and Philipstown. The plantation was not a great success, but the towns survived to become more prosperous in the next century. Maryborough is now known as Port Laoise and Philipstown is called Daingean.

## MUNSTER

### THE PLANTATION OF MUNSTER

The province of Munster was in a state of war and rebellion down to 1583, when the second Desmond rebellion was crushed. The government of Queen Elizabeth I decided to try a different kind of plantation to Leix and Offaly. Instead of government money being used to pay for the plantation, the province was divided up into parcels of land which were let to 'undertakers' who undertook to implement plantation *using their own money*.

These 'undertakers' included many famous Englishmen, such as Sir Walter Raleigh and the poet Edmund Spenser. Settlers came from many western British counties; a number of new towns were built and old ports were restored. However, there were too few settlers, and the plantation was not a great success.

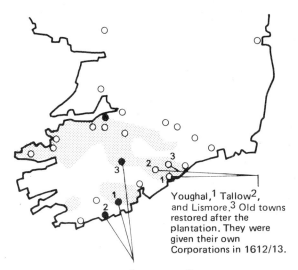

Youghal,[1] Tallow[2], and Lismore.[3] Old towns restored after the plantation. They were given their own Corporations in 1612/13.

Bandon,[1] Clonakilty[2] and Mallow.[3] Three towns founded after the plantation of Munster.

 PLANTED AREAS
O   OLD TOWNS
●   NEW TOWNS

---

*Opposite - Cahir Castle, Co. Tipperary under attack in 1599 by troops under the Earl of Essex, from a contemporary drawing.*

The main lesson learned from the Munster plantation was that a plantation needed more towns if it was to be successful. In 1609, after the Gaelic lords of Ulster were defeated in the Nine Years' War and had left the country, their lands were taken over by the Crown. By 1641 a new network of 16 towns had been built throughout the province. However, the 'towns' were unevenly spread, and only three, Strabane, Derry and Coleraine, were of any real size.

The rebellion of 1641 showed how vulnerable the new Ulster towns were to attack, and many settlers were killed. However, the plantations of Ulster changed the face of Irish history, and most of the towns established under the plantation are still of major importance.

The plantation of Ulster of 1609 involved six counties, Donegal, Derry, Tyrone, Armagh, Fermanagh and Cavan. The plans provided for plantation by new settlers and Irish.

Antrim and Down had been colonised by Gaelic-speaking Scots from the Hebrides. They were also granted to a variety of Scots and English undertakers.

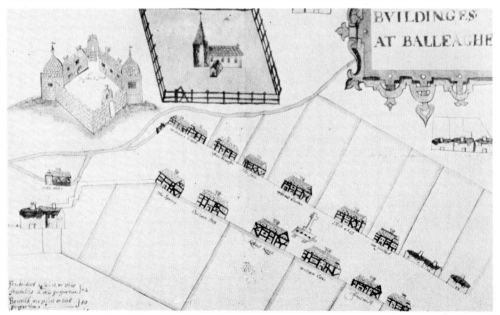

*The village of Bellaghy, Co. Derry from a plan dated 1622. Planters' names are written beside their houses, which are of the timber-frame type. Note the mill on the river and, in the middle of the street, the village cross. The stocks underneath were used to punish those found guilty of small offences.*

# CHANGES IN IRISH TOWNS 1550-1700

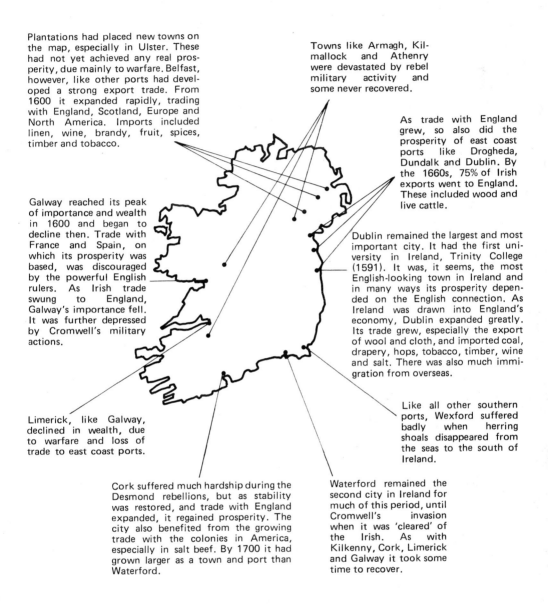

Plantations had placed new towns on the map, especially in Ulster. These had not yet achieved any real prosperity, due mainly to warfare. Belfast, however, like other ports had developed a strong export trade. From 1600 it expanded rapidly, trading with England, Scotland, Europe and North America. Imports included linen, wine, brandy, fruit, spices, timber and tobacco.

Galway reached its peak of importance and wealth in 1600 and began to decline then. Trade with France and Spain, on which its prosperity was based, was discouraged by the powerful English rulers. As Irish trade swung to England, Galway's importance fell. It was further depressed by Cromwell's military actions.

Limerick, like Galway, declined in wealth, due to warfare and loss of trade to east coast ports.

Cork suffered much hardship during the Desmond rebellions, but as stability was restored, and trade with England expanded, it regained prosperity. The city also benefited from the growing trade with the colonies in America, especially in salt beef. By 1700 it had grown larger as a town and port than Waterford.

Towns like Armagh, Kilmallock and Athenry were devastated by rebel military activity and some never recovered.

As trade with England grew, so also did the prosperity of east coast ports like Drogheda, Dundalk and Dublin. By the 1660s, 75% of Irish exports went to England. These included wood and live cattle.

Dublin remained the largest and most important city. It had the first university in Ireland, Trinity College (1591). It was, it seems, the most English-looking town in Ireland and in many ways its prosperity depended on the English connection. As Ireland was drawn into England's economy, Dublin expanded greatly. Its trade grew, especially the export of wool and cloth, and imported coal, drapery, hops, tobacco, timber, wine and salt. There was also much immigration from overseas.

Like all other southern ports, Wexford suffered badly when herring shoals disappeared from the seas to the south of Ireland.

Waterford remained the second city in Ireland for much of this period, until Cromwell's invasion when it was 'cleared' of the Irish. As with Kilkenny, Cork, Limerick and Galway it took some time to recover.

The two most important factors that affected the growth of Irish towns in this period were warfare and trade. Rebellions in Munster and Ulster in the 16th century, the rebellion of 1691, followed by Cromwell's savage suppression, and the Williamite War of 1689—91 which finally established the Protestant ascendancy, all kept much of the country and many towns in ruins. When peace was restored, however, trade grew again, and Ireland began to export to Britain and the new colonies in America.

## DERRY — A Plantation Town

Derry was an ancient settlement in a fine location on Lough Foyle. In 1600 Sir Henry Dowcra placed a small garrison there, and a decade later the building of the town began. A typical plantation town, it had strong walls and a geometrical layout, with the two main streets meeting in 'The Diamond'. The houses were of timber or stone, often several storeys high, roofed with slate and with glass windows.

Derry rapidly became an important trading centre, with a loyal Protestant population of merchants, shopkeepers and craftsmen. The people of Derry showed their loyalty to the Protestant cause in 1689, when the city was besieged for 105 days by the army of the Catholic King of England, James II. Great hardship was endured until a relief ship forced its way through on 30th July 1689. The anniversary of the city's relief is still celebrated by the loyalist population.

By 1786, Derry had spread well beyond its walls, after almost a century of peace. Its fine harbour and location on Lough Foyle made it the most important trading centre in the north-west of Ireland, and it served a very large area, including much of the counties Donegal, Derry and Tyrone.

In the early 19th century it expanded further, and one writer described how 'up river and down the estuary, the slopes and heights are adorned by handsome villas'. Its main industries were flour-milling, brewing and distilling. In the town centre stood the courthouse and a fine Protestant Cathedral.

The great Famine of 1845-9, which re-shaped the face of most of Ireland, had less impact on the north, which was wealthier and more heavily industrialised. By 1901 Derry had a population of over 33,000. It had become the centre of a home and factory-based shirt industry, its port had links with Britain and America for both passengers and freight.

After Northern Ireland became a self-governing state in 1922, Derry's prosperity declined. It was ruled by a Unionist minority, and their sectarian politics ensured poor employment and housing for Roman Catholics. The Northern Ireland Civil Rights movement of the 1960s drew attention to these problems and local government was reformed in 1969. By then, however, events in Northern Ireland had begun the steady drift into armed conflict that has continued through the 1970s into the 1980s.

*The City of Derry in 1686.*

*Derry city as seen through Bishop's Gate, part of the original city wall.*

# The Georgian Town

By 1700 peace was restored in Ireland, and the country was firmly in the grip of law and order. For the first time ever, townspeople no longer had to fear attack from the hills around their towns. They could build houses outside the walls, and plan new wide streets stretching into the suburbs. There was a new feeling for town planning and famous architects came to Ireland to design gracious new buildings for the ruling class. It was fashionable to see ancient Greece and Rome as the roots of civilisation, and many of the new buildings were designed to echo the splendours of these old cities.

The new streets were broad and the houses were built of stone and brick. Building grew in importance as an industry. In Waterford the Exchange, the Customs House and the Courthouse were built; in Belfast there was the Linen-hall, and in Limerick the Assembly Rooms and the Georgian area of Newtown Pery.

Trade brought prosperity for some. Woollen yarn was exported in bulk and important spinning centres grew up in Dublin, and especially in Cork, where half the wool in Ireland was combed. It is also said that huge quantities of wool were smuggled to Europe from the south-west and west.

There was also a thriving trade in salted beef, pork and butter to Europe and the West Indies, especially from Cork and Waterford. This trade also brought prosperity to the midlands, where the cattle came from, and established other industries such as tanning and tallow-making.

The largest export was linen, which was concentrated in Ulster. It was a cottage industry. Most northern towns had linen-markets, where the woven cloth was sold. Afterwards it was bleached and then exported. Linen was exported from the north, through Derry, Newry and Belfast, and overland to Dublin.

Among the other industries that were to be found throughout Ireland were milling, brewing and distilling, as well as the manufacture of articles such as pots, kettles and spades. The majority of the people, however, lived in the country, and as the population grew through the 18th century, very many lived in awful poverty.

The same squalor was to be found in most towns and cities. In the tenements of Georgian Ireland, violence and poverty were commonplace. In Limerick in 1771, for example, a crowd attacked a flour-mill and was only driven off by gun-fire. By 1841 towns were crowded with the poor and destitute, many

*Fire-fighting remains a priority of any city administration.*

## To the COMMITTEE for conducting the FREE-PRESS.

GENTLEMEN,

AS I look upon your Paper as the beft Channel thro' which public Grievances may be fo expofed as to call for immediate Redrefs, I beg Leave to lay before you a Grievance, with which this City is threatened, of the moft dangerous and deftructive Nature to the Health and to the Trade of the Inhabitants of this City.

The Grievance I mean, is that of preparing to burn a large Quantity of Bricks between St. Martin's-lane and Summer-hill; a Situation, from its Circumftances, the moft likely to infeft the neighbouring Buildings, I may fay all the City, with that moft noxious Vapour which arifes from burning Clay.

The Perfon engaged in this deftructive Work feems quite unmoved at the Deftruction and Defolation for which he is thus preparing.

He has been applied to by all the Inhabitants of the Neighbourhood; the evil Confequences of fuch a Work were all clearly laid before him; but he remained quite unmoved by the moft affecting Remonftrances. When all Confiderations of this Nature proved ineffectual, the heinous Offence againft the Public, the Nature of the Nuifance was explained to him, and Notice was given him of a firm Refolution of the Inhabitants to put the Laws in Force, to the Punifhment of this deftructive Offence.

But the intended Offender was as little moved by Threats of condign Punifhment, as with the Motives of Humanity laid open upon the firft Application againft this deftructive Nuifance: He treated both with equal Contempt. He faid, he had bought the Ground, it was his Property, and he would put it to what Ufe he found moft to his private Advantage, regardlefs of all ill Confequences to the Public.

Sackville - ftreet,
April 2. 1766.

Yours, &c.
A CITIZEN.

*Letter of complaint published 1766.*

*The Four Courts on the Liffey, one of Dublin's splendid Georgian buildings.*

of them fleeing the dire poverty of the countryside.

The situation was worse in some areas than others. Those fortunate enough to have an 'improving landlord' had workers trained for some industry, and fine new buildings erected, sometimes even whole new villages or towns. In the south, Blarney, Killarney and Fermoy were built or re-built this way, as were Clifden and Belmullet in the west, in the 19th century.

### THE NEW DUBLIN

It was during the reign of the Georges that massive plans for a new Dublin were drawn up and carried out. Georgian Dublin spread from the old medieval walls to the sea. It was a residential city for a wealthy class that believed that cities were the centre of civilised society.

In 1660 only 9,000 people lived in Dublin and many of its buildings were derelict. The City Assembly met to consider how this poor and ruinous town could become a worthy capital of a proud kingdom. It was decided that little could be done with what existed, so that a new start would have to be made. The land chosen was that of St. Stephen's Green, open grazing land to the east of the city. A rectangle with sides almost a quarter of a mile in length was measured out, a roadway laid around it, and the lands facing the green divided into building plots and let to the business people of the town. They had to build to certain standards and plant trees in the open space opposite their plots.

The houses opposite are typical of built during this period of expansion in Dublin. They are upper-class houses. Usually they had kitchens and a laundry room in the basement, the main hall and 'reception' rooms on the ground floor, special rooms (e.g. music room) and family bedrooms upstairs, and servants' rooms, and sewing room, etc. on the upper floor. The rooms were very large, and the best houses had beautiful decorative plasterwork on the ceilings and fine marble fireplaces in the main rooms. Usually these features were found on the lower floors, the upper storeys being less carefully designed. Outside the main features were the doorways, the many-paned windows and the wrought-iron railings. These homes of the wealthy were designed to please the eye in a quiet way. The windows and doors were built to suit the size of the building, so that the whole house looked well, no matter what size it was.

St. Stephen's Green was the first of many developments. The city grew on both sides of the Liffey. The biggest developer on each bank gave their names to streets they laid out — Luke Gardiner to the north, and Lord Fitzwilliam to the south. In 1795 Carlisle Bridge joined the two estates

*The Wide-Street Commissioners were given the task to plan the new city of Dublin.*

directly, and fashionable Dubliners could visit friends across the river

*An early view of Dublin from Phoenix Park.*

without venturing upriver to the less splendid districts close to the old city walls.

The new planners were convinced that every great city should have splendid public buildings. A new Custom House was planned downriver from the old, but the merchants and people of the old city knew that if it was built there, trade would no longer reach the old quays. Crowds rioted at the new site and tried to fill in the foundation trenches. The protest failed, and classical splendour arose on the sloblands reclaimed behind the quay wall.

As soon as the building was finished, the old city was cut off from the sea by Carlisle Bridge. Ships sailing into Dublin had the benefit of the greatest public work undertaken since the building of the city walls — the construction of the North and South Walls to prevent the silting-up of the harbour entrance. This project was begun in 1707 by the Ballast Office, set up by the Corporation to improve the port. The four-mile long South Wall was completed and Poolbeg

lighthouse begun in 1762. The slobland behind the walls was reclaimed; before this, high tides could reach as far inland as the lands of Trinity College.

The growing prosperity of the city filled the streets with carts bringing goods to and from the port. In Georgian Dublin the manufacturing quarter was in the older part of Dublin known as the Liberties. The area had a very successful brewing industry, and a large textile industry. Workshops making coaches, silverware, and luxury goods for the wealthier classes employed skilled workers and craftsmen. The houses and shops of the rich employed large numbers of servants.

Life among the poor was not easy. The old quarter was deserted by the wealthy. Ferocious street battles were common, often between the Protestant weavers of the Liberties and the Catholic butchers from the Ormonde meat market across the river. People, even children, were hanged for the theft of small items. It was believed that such vicious justice was necessary to preserve civilised life from the barbarous cruelty and depravity of the mob.

The Phoenix Park was also the site of duels, bull-baiting and cock-fighting, and of military reviews which were a popular spectacle, as were the public executions at St. Stephen's Green and Kilmainham. The poor could also sit in the cheapest seats of theatres, of which Smock Alley was the best known. Unpopular actors and plays were pelted with rotten fruit, and there were frequent riots.

There were also numerous literary and debating societies. The Royal Irish Academy was founded in 1785 to encourage the study of science, Irish history and archaeology.

There was, however, one great development in Dublin which served all its people — the securing for public use of the Phoenix Park. In 1662, while plans were being laid for building on St. Stephen's Green to the east, the Viceroy began to buy land to add to the demesne surrounding the Vice-Regal residence. Bit by bit the lands of the present park were bought for a royal deer park, open to the public. It was called Phoenix, from the Irish words 'Fionn Uisce', for the spring which rises in the park. It was walled from the beginning, provided with rangers, and the lakes were created at the city end. The rich were to live in classical splendour away from the medievel squalor, and the poor could at least think of a pleasant stroll in the park as their version of the new ideal of city life.

Ireland was a kingdom in 1800, newly united to Great Britain in the United Kingdom of Great Britain and Ireland, with its own aristocracy, a titled landowning ruling class, many of whom built great houses in Dublin during the Georgian period. They were the largest private houses ever built in Ireland. Many have since become public buildings, such as Leinster House, shown here.

*Leinster House, once one of the great family houses of the 18th century. Lord Edward Fitzgerald was born here in 1763. It is now Dáil Éireann.*

### A Traveller in Dublin, 1834

'First impressions of Dublin are decidedly favourable. Entering from Kingstown, there is little to be seen that is unworthy the approach to a capital, and without passing through any of those wretched suburbs which stretch in many other directions, one is whirled at once into a magnificent centre, where there is an assemblage of all that usually gives evidence of wealth and taste, and of the existence of a great and flourishing city.

A stranger arriving in Dublin in spring, as I did, will be struck even less by the architectural beauty of the city than by other kinds of splendour: I allude to the indulgences of luxury, and the apparent proofs of wealth that are everywhere thrust upon the eye — the numerous private vehicles that fill the streets, and even blockade many of them; the magnificent shops for the sale of articles of luxury and taste, at the doors of which, in Grafton Street, I have counted upwards of twenty handsome equipages; and in certain quarters of the city, the number of splendid homes, and 'legion' of liveried servants. But a little closer observation and more minute inquiry, will in some measure correct these impressions; and will bring to mind the well-known and well-founded proverb that 'it is not all gold that glitters' . . .

In walking through the streets of Dublin, strange and striking contrasts are presented between grandeur and poverty. In Merrion Square, St. Stephen's Green and elsewhere, the ragged wretches that are sitting on the steps, contrast strongly with the splendour of the houses and the magnificent equipages that wait without: pass from Merrion Square or Grafton Street, about three o'clock, into what is called the Liberty, and you might easily fancy yourself in another and distant part of Europe. . .

In London every fifth or sixth shop is a bacon and cheese-shop. In Dublin, luxuries of a different kind offer their temptations. What would be the use of opening a bacon shop, where the lower orders, who are elsewhere the chief purchasers of bacon, cannot afford to eat bacon and live upon potatoes?

As I have mentioned the lower orders in Dublin, I may add that from the house in which I lived in Kildare Street, being exactly opposite to the Royal Dublin Society, which was then exhibiting a cattle-show, I was very favourably situated for observing, among the crowd collected, some of those little traits which throw light upon character and condition. I remarked in particular the great eagerness of everyone to get a little employment, and earn a penny or two. I observed another less equivocal proof of low condition. After the cattle had been fed, the half-eaten turnips became the perquisite of the crowd of ragged boys and girls outside. Many and fierce were the scrambles for these precious relics; and a half-gnawed turnip, when once secured, was guarded with the most vigilant jealousy, and was lent for a mouthful to another longing tatter-demalion, as much apparently as an act of extraordinary favour, as if the root had been a pineapple.'

*Henry Inglis: Ireland in 1834*

# TOWNS OF IRELAND 1841

Sligo was the regional centre for the north west. Its trade was larger than Galway and was mainly agricultural. There were four breweries, a distillery, flour mills and some smaller industries, such as soap, tobacco, and ropes.

Derry was expanding. As a port, it served a huge area from Donegal to the Sperrin Mountains.

Belfast had become the country's second port, and a rapidly expanding industrial centre. New docks were built and exports increased. There were many flax-spinning mills, and other industries. The foundations were also being laid for the ship-building industry. Above all, it was gifted with some very astute businessmen. The Lagan Valley was becoming a major industrial area.

Galway's port trade was growing in agricultural produce. Fishing was of great importance. Other industries included brewing, paper, ironwork, tanning and rope-making. It had regional, bustling markets.

Drogheda,[1] Dundalk,[2] and Newry[3] were three successful east coast towns. Drogheda was the largest with a large agricultural export trade. It had a cotton mill, and other industries included leather, footwear, soap, candles, and brewing. All the same, there was also much poverty.

Dublin was still the main port, market and administrative centre. Road and rail systems met in the city, as did the canals. It had, however, lost much of its former grandeur when Ireland was united with Great Britain in the United Kingdom.

Most of Limerick's exports were agricultural, as were its industries. Linen-weaving had declined.

Tralee was the largest town in Kerry, and had been greatly improved by the landlord. It had a thriving port, exporting agricultural produce.

Wexford's main industry was malting barley for the Dublin market. It also had a distillery, breweries and a ropeworks, and its port was active in importing and exporting.

Kilkenny was still the chief inland town and a major market centre. However, like many inland towns its industries were failing and there was much poverty.

Cork, the third city was the major port of the south. It exported agricultural produce from the fertile lands of Cork, Limerick and east Kerry. The British Navy took on supplies there, and the city also supplied the Transatlantic ships. It had a wide number of industries.

Waterford drew trade from a wide area in the south east by road and boat, along the Suir and the Barrow and its canals.

In 1841, only five towns had more than 20,000 people, and all five were ports. Of the thirteen with populations of 10,000 to 20,000, eight were ports. In general economic activity had not changed greatly over the preceding centuries. Agriculture was still the mainstay of Irish town life, in the export, or sale, or processing of agricultural produce. Bacon-curing, butter-selling, leather-working, brewing and distilling were the kinds of industries found in most towns. Poverty was very common, especially in the west. The major exceptions to the gloomy picture was the north east, where an industrial revolution was beginning.

# Irish Towns 1841~1980

In 1841 only 20 per cent of the people of Ireland lived in towns. By 1971 59 per cent of the population of the Republic and 55 per cent of the population of Northern Ireland, lived in towns. Strangely enough, however, many towns experienced no growth, and some fell into decline. The population of Carrick-on-Suir fell by 55 per cent in that period, for example, and the once-thriving medieval port of Youghal by 43 per cent.

The key to understanding the figures is the great Famine, which changed the face of Ireland. The west of Ireland was devastated, and emigration became a constant drain on all the country. The Land War of the 1880s, famines and rebellion all helped to depress trade and industry in the south.

From the Famine until the 1960s, industry remained based on agricultural produce. While linen mills, textile factories, bacon-curing, tanning, brewing, distilling and livestock sales brought prosperity to some country towns, most of them remained small. The largest towns, as ever, were ports.

The only exception to this rather gloomy picture was the north-east of the country, which experienced an industrial revolution like many British cities. By the year 1901 Belfast had grown as large as Dublin. Its growth was based on the success of the shipbuilding and linen industries.

Although trade and industry were run down in many parts of Ireland, there were some notable additions to the list of Irish towns during the 19th and 20th centuries:

*Railway Terminus, Queenstown (Cobh).*

## RAILWAY TOWNS

When the railway network was being planned, many old and well-established towns were included on the lines, such as Drogheda, Dundalk, Athlone and Limerick. The planners had to link the major centres with one another, after all, since one of the aims of the railway was to move goods rapidly from place to place.

Yet, each line involved a decision on where to go. The first plans for the northern railway suggested that it should go through Navan, and Armagh. Instead, it went through Drogheda and Portadown. Undoubtedly, there were good reasons for the choices — Drogheda was a large and successful port, for example. The decision brought prosperity to the towns chosen and left the others to develop as best they could.

Elsewhere the railways went further, creating, in the case of Bray and Greystones for example, railway towns. The entire shape of Dublin was changed, as the middle and upper classes availed of the opportunity to live by the sea and take the train to the city for work. The coast from Dublin to Greystones was rapidly incorporated into the city. Kingstown, now known as Dun Laoghaire, expanded rapidly, due also to the presence of its steamship harbour. Cobh in Co. Cork, a port-of-call for transatlantic steamers, and linked to Cork by rail, was another southern town that owed its growth to steam-power.

## RESORT TOWNS

The 19th century saw a growing fashion for people to take holidays by the seaside, travelling, for the most part by rail. Dun Laoghaire, Bray and Greystones were all popular resorts for Dubliners. In the south there was Tramore, in the north Kilkeel, Warrenpoint, Donaghadee, Bangor, Portrush and Portstewart, and in Donegal, Bundoran was popular. Older towns also began to attract visitors, and all around the country a tourist trade began to develop.

In particular, Ireland's beauty spots became famous, such as Killarney, where a town founded by an 'improving landlord' grew ito a famous resort.

## MILITARY TOWNS

In the 16th century most of Ireland's towns had garrisons quartered in them. Later, however, the military tended to be found only in certain 'garrison towns'. Athlone had a large barracks, as had Dundalk. Dublin was ringed with military housing. Cobh in Co. Cork, had a large number of gun emplacements, defensive positions and naval bases.

## INDUSTRIAL TOWNS

Many of the old plantation towns in Ulster grew large in the 19th century as the province's industrial strength grew. Lisburn, Lurgan, Derry, Newtownards and Ballymena all expanded very rapidly as the textile and engineering industries developed.

This rapid growth and industrial development needed large numbers of workers, and a new style of housing for them: small, family dwellings, cheap enough to be rented by a working man, were built in the shadow of the factories.

The 20th century has seen Ulster's industrial revolution run aground, with widespread unemployment in many towns. In the late 20th century the province's heavy industry found it difficult to compete with Japanese shipbuilding and the Asian textile industry.

*Industrial Housing.*

Although the rest of Ireland has also suffered from under-employment, there the similarity ends. A new industrial revolution was launched in the 1960s to provide employment for the rapidly growing population. New industrial estates were located in towns all over Ireland. Smaller towns are not growing; but large centres are. Dublin, which grew very slowly in the 19th century, is now the fastest-growing region, with one-quarter of the total population of Ireland. It has long ago swallowed up small villages that lay near it, and neighbouring towns such as Lucan, Maynooth and, especially, Dun Laoghaire have expanded until they are among the largest towns in Ireland.

New 'satellite towns' are planned to cater for the vast population explosion in the Greater Dublin Region, at Tallaght, Clondalkin and Blanchardstown. These will each have a population of about 100,000. Unlike much of the uncontrolled growth that has taken place so far, however, the new towns are being planned as such and will incorporate industrial estates into their layout. The first such industrial town in the Republic was built at Shannon in the 1960s. In Northern Ireland there are two such new towns, at Newtown-abbey, north of Belfast, and at Craigavon, linking the older town of Portadown and Lurgan into one super-town.

# NEW IRISH TOWNS 1800-1980

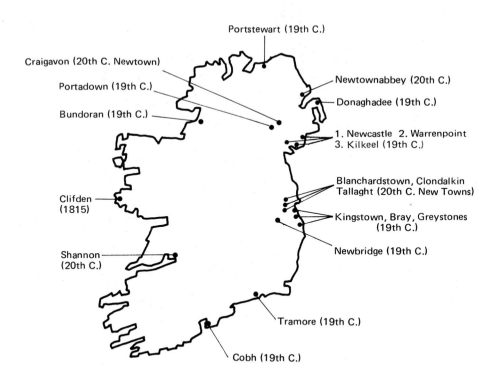

Portstewart (19th C.)

Craigavon (20th C. Newtown)

Portadown (19th C.)

Bundoran (19th C.)

Newtownabbey (20th C.)

Donaghadee (19th C.)

1. Newcastle  2. Warrenpoint
3. Kilkeel (19th C.)

Clifden
(1815)

Blanchardstown, Clondalkin
Tallaght (20th C. New Towns)

Kingstown, Bray, Greystones
(19th C.)

Newbridge (19th C.)

Shannon
(20th C.)

Tramore (19th C.)

Cobh (19th C.)

*Bray, Co. Wicklow, a 19th century resort town made popular by the railway.*

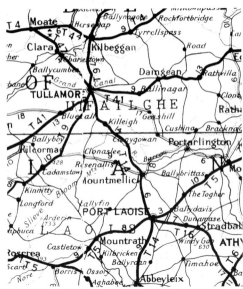

Philipstown, now known as Daingean, was a Tudor plantation town. For several hundred years it was an important centre in Co. Offaly, Tullamore, although established around the same time, was mainly an estate town of the 18th century. It began to expand rapidly in 1799 when the Grand Canal reached the town. From 1804, when the canal reached the Shannon, Tullamore became a strong market centre, and completely superseded Philipstown, which became a mere village.

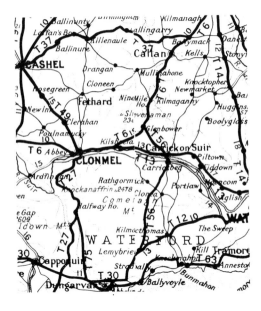

Armagh was an important town in 1841, with flour and corn mills, breweries, distilleries and tanneries, with few poor houses. Over the later 19th century, however, it was out-shone by its neighbour Portadown, which expanded rapidly when the railway was built. It was a major junction on the Belfast-Dublin line. Armagh remained a market and residential town, while Portadown became an important industrial centre.

By the 1830s the woollen trade in Carrick-on-Suir had ceased and the town had deteriorated into disrepair and poverty. Clonmel, a mere 21 kilometres away, was doing well, even though it too had lost its woollen industry. However, road and river transport met in Clonmel, and its warehouses were filled with grain, butter and bacon, to be carried by road or river to Waterford for export. Other industries were bacon-curing, flour-milling and cotton-weaving. It was a court and garrison town, and housed the headquarters of the Bianconi car services.

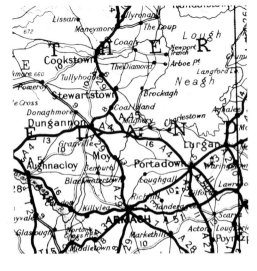

*Part Three*

# THE NEW INDUSTRIAL SOCIETY: CASE STUDIES OF CHANGE

# A Local World

Two hundred years ago people lived in a local, highly familiar world. The neighbourhood or parish was very important; most people were likely to live out their lives in the place where they were born, marry there and be buried there.

Work was on the farm, in the home or in domestic industries; even in towns, places of work were local and personal. Transport was usually by foot, or horse for longer distances; a journey of some length to and from work every day would have been unheard of. The way of life did not change greatly from one generation to the next. Michael McGowan, for example, was born in 1865 into a world untouched by outside influences:

'It's not easy for this generation to understand the circumstances of life as they were when I was young. Often now, as I think back over life as it was then, I feel as if I'm dreaming.

Life was untroubled enough in the manner of the times and the people were content even if they didn't think so then. Neither turmoil nor tumult, on sea or on land, existed to disturb them. Neither books nor papers were available to them; they were unlearnt and untaught and they were never troubled by any convulsions in the great world outside. If they had to go from home they went on foot but that didn't give them a day's worry. Hardly more than two people in the whole parish had a clock, and if they had to look to being punctual — which was seldom — they relied on the sun or on the moon. To make a long story short, it was little they had to do with the world outside except for the news that a travelling man would bring them from time to time.'

*from The Hard Road to Klondyke*

In the century that followed, new inventions and discoveries resulted in the development of new machine technology. It was what these new

*North Strand, Dublin, in the early 19th century.*

*Belfast, early 20th century.*

machines could do — large-scale manufacture, speedy means of transport, instant communication over long distances, for example — which brought about such radical changes in how people lived.

Historians often refer to the developments which took place during this period as 'revolutions', because of the profound and far-reaching effects they had. They were closely linked; developments in one area caused developments in another. For example, growing industries, based on factory production, needed more efficient transport systems to serve them; at the same time the building of transport networks such as railways and canals would have brought about new industrial developments.

This chapter looks at some of these 'revolutions' and at how they have formed the basis of modern urban life.

# Industry

If you were to compare a picture of a city street in 1800 with one from 1900, the most important difference might not be visible. Certainly, you would see evidence of new technology, especially in transport, but the real difference would be that in 1900 almost everything would have been made in a new way, whether it looked different or not. In the hundred years between the two pictures, machine technology and the factory system had taken over from the traditional ways of manufacture.

Up to the new industrial age every-

*Domestic industry.*

thing had been made by hand, with simple tools at home, or in small workshops. Heavier work was done with the help of animals, or simple machines powered by wind or moving water. The produce of the land provided the raw materials for industry, barley for brewing and distilling, wheat for the mills and wool and flax for the manufacture of cloth.

There was an even closer connection between farming and industry. Most farmers were also part-time industrial workers. What is known as *domestic industry* was found all over Ireland and England at this time. Around the end of the 18th century, for example, there would have been a spinning wheel in many cabins in the country. While the woman of the house looked after the spinning, her husband was a part-time weaver. Any yarn or cloth sold provided the money which helped pay the rent or buy simple luxuries like tobacco, clay pipes, snuff, salt and shop whiskey.

The late 18th century saw the development of machines which made it possible for one worker to do the

job of many, even hundreds. With these machines, driven by foot or hand-operated mechanisms, the basis for the factory system was laid.

Using an external source of power to operate the machinery was only a step away from this. It was not a new idea; water-power had been used to operate simple machinery, for example corn-mills, for thousands of years. Using the same principle, the flow of water was now harnessed and used to operate the machinery of the new factories, which had to be built near rivers. By the beginning of the 19th century, enormous water-wheels — some more than 10 metres in diameter — were a common sight on Irish and British rivers. Power from the water-wheels was transmitted by wheels and gears to the factory mechanisms.

However, wheels could only turn as fast as the water flowed, and hand- or foot-operated machines could only go as fast as the human body. It was really the discovery of a new source of power that brought about the

*Mill-races were specially built to make a river flow faster. This one is on a County Cork river.*

## NEWCOMEN'S ENGINE

The cylinder (1) was placed directly above the boiler (2). A piston (3) was attached to one end of the rocking beam (4). The pump-rod (5) was at the other end of the beam.

Steam was let in at atmospheric pressure at the bottom of the cylinder. The piston rose. A jet of cold water (6) would then quickly condense the steam in the sealed cylinder, creating a vacuum. This drew the piston back down. Letting in new steam would restart the cycle.

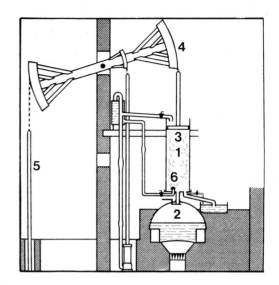

Industrial Revolution. This source of power was steam.

### THE STEAM AGE

In 1709 Thomas Newcomen invented the first steam engine. It was a machine with an up-and-down motion, and was used to pump water from coalmines.

The 'fire engine' for raising water was cumbersome, slow, but very useful. In the 1870s one was built into a newly sunk coalmine in East Tyrone; it was Ireland's first steam-engine on record.

Newcomen's engine set many people thinking about the further potential of steam. In 1781 James Watt built an engine which used steam at high pressure to rotate a wheel. The great water-wheels on the banks of many rivers in the country were now to compete for business with the power of steam.

Once steam engines were put to work to drive the machinery of the textile industry, it became clear just what steam-power could do. From this beginning a whole new engineering developed which was to revolutionise industry, especially the manufacture of iron and steel. Coal became all-important, and in coalfields all over Britain great factories were built.

The new technology did not put the workers in the longer established industries, such as textiles, out of a job. Far from it. Although the heavy plants could do work which, would have once needed thousands of people, production increased so much that there was plenty of work for everyone, manual craftsmen and traditional industrial workers alike. It was the *nature* of their work that had changed.

Mass-production meant that each worker had a small, repetitive task to do somewhere along the line of pro-

## REQUIEM FOR A MILL

They took away the water-wheel,
Scrap-ironed all the corn-mill;
The water now cascades with no
Audience pacing to and fro
Taking in with casual glance
Experience.

The cold wet blustery winter day
And all that's happening will stay
Alive in the mind: the bleak
Water-flushed meadows speak
An enduring story
To a man indifferent in a doorway.

Packaged, precooked flakes have left
A land of this old mill bereft.
The ghosts that were so local coloured
Hiding behind bags of pollard
Have gone from those empty walls.
The weir still curves its waterfalls
But lets them drop in the tailrace
No longer wholly chivalrous.

And with this mention we withdraw
To things above the temporal law.

*Patrick Kavanagh*

duction; there was little contact between the people involved in different stages of production and few workers had anything to do with the finished product. The pace of work was set by the power-driven machinery and had to be kept up.

The new industries drew a distinct line between home and work — work was carried out in one place, home life and leisure in another. This was to be an important factor in the way towns and cities developed from then on.

### THE INDUSTRIAL REVOLUTION
### IN BRITAIN

Britain was the first society to undergo these changes. The Industrial Revolution began there in the second half of the 18th century and was well advanced by the 1840s. It spread to Europe but had little impact in Ireland. Ireland, in fact, never had an Industrial Revolution in the sense that Britain had.

Many factors existed in Britain at

'Merino Factory, County of Kilkenny, founded in the Year 1810, by Messrs. Nowlan & Shaw, for the purpose of establishing the manufacture of superfine cloth in Ireland, and of providing employment and education for its industrious poor.'

*Roe's Distillery, Thomas Street, Dublin, c.1878. Distilling and brewing were Dublin's most important industries.*

the time, which would have both caused and encouraged the Industrial Revolution there:

- The rising population forced people to leave the land and created a steady supply of workers for industry.
- Improved farming methods meant that there were fewer jobs in rural areas, but also provided food to feed the growing population in towns and cities.
- The invention of new machinery and, in particular, the discovery of steam as a source of power, increased production and introduced many new goods.
- The expanding British Empire and growth of overseas trade provided Britain with a market for the output of her factories.
- Improved transport, through the growth of railways and steamships, allowed for the fast movement of people, goods and ideas.

- Britain had large deposits of iron ore, which was the raw material used in iron and steel manufacturing, while her deposits of coal provided the power for the expanding industry.

The new factories had to be built near their source of power. The coalfields of the north and midlands in Britain became the location of the new towns and cities, which grew rapidly as people travelled to them in search of work. England became known as the workshop of the world, and became the world's first modern industrial state.

The textile industry was only one of many in which the new technology was applied. Metal-working and engineering were revolutionised by machine tools. Pottery became a huge factory industry, as did flour-milling, soap-making and many others. Everywhere old relations of production gave way to new.

## TEXTILE INDUSTRY

| | Under the domestic system | Under the Factory System |
|---|---|---|
| Raw material | Locally-produced fibres — e.g. wool and flax — would either be supplied by contractors or be the product of the spinners' own lands. | Locally-produced fibres were no longer sufficient in quantity for the new system of production. Plentiful and cheap sources were available abroad — e.g. raw cotton produced by slave labour on American plantations — and improved transport systems made these accessible. |
| Spinning | Spinning by hand was very laborious and it took several spinners to supply one weaver. The work was usually done at home, often by many members of the family. | Earlier spinning machines were worked by water power. With the development of the steam engine, huge mills were built near coalfields (e.g. in Lancashire), spinning for the home market or for export via the Liverpool docks. Water wheels could not compete, and the cloth-making industry became highly concentrated in particular areas. |
| Weaving | Weavers collected yarn from the spinners. Often they had to make long journeys through mountainous countries to collect the yarn they needed for one season's weaving. Looms were hand- or foot-operated. | With the development of the power-loom, factories were set up to weave the produce of the spinning mills. There was now no contact between the workers at both stages of production, for the product belonged to the machine (and to its owner) and not to the operator. |
| Distribution | Before the Industrial Revolution there was already a strong cloth-making industry. Cloth was widely traded and highly valued. Different cloth types had different markets, but most of the hard-wearing fabrics for everyday clothes were produced locally. | With the Industrial Revolution, distribution was world wide. Cloth produced in the industrialised nations seized the trade of the world, impoverishing workers in the domestic clothmaking in other countries. The industrialised nations began to exploit the rural world in a new and devastating way. |

### STEAM POWER AND BEER MAKING

'Last summer we set up a steam engine for the purpose of grinding our malt. It is built in the place where the mill-houses used to stand with the malt loft over them . . . .

Our wheel, you may remember, required six horses to turn it, but we ordered our engine the power of ten, and the work it does we think is equal to fourteen horses, for we grind with all our four mills about forty qrs. an hour, besides raising the liquor. We began this season's work with it, and have now ground about twenty-eight thousand qrs. without accident or interruption. Its great uses and advantages give us all great satisfaction and are daily pointed out afresh to us.'

*Joseph Delafield, Assistant to Samuel Whitbread Brewers, in a letter c. 1785.*

### WEAVING BY MACHINE

'Before the invention of the dressing

frame, one weaver was required to each steam loom; at present a boy or girl, fourteen or fifteen years of age, can manage two steam looms, and with their help can weave three and a half times as much cloth as the best hand weaver. The best hand weavers seldom produce a piece of uniform evenness; indeed, it is next to impossible for them to do so, because a weaker or stronger blow with the lathe immediately alters the thickness of the cloth. In steam looms, the lathe gives a steady, certain blow, and once regulated by the engineer, moves with the greatest precision from the beginning to the end of the piece.'

*Richard Guest, in his Compendious History of the Cotton Manufacture, 1823.*

## MANUFACTURING INDUSTRY IN IRELAND

The Industrial Revolution made little impact on the development of industry in most of Ireland. The country lacked the resources of coal and iron, the landlord system left little money for investment, there was a declining population, and it was difficult to compete with low-priced English goods.

The only area to undergo a pattern of growth that compared with Britain's industrial towns was the Lagan Valley around Belfast. The north-east of Ireland had the advantages of being close to the Clyde industrial area in Scotland, and coal and iron were easily imported. The relationship between landlord and tenant was better there than elsewhere, and there was more capital available for investment. The traditional linen factories were fitted with steam-powered weaving machinery.

Rope, cotton, canvas, tweed and furniture soon became important industries in the region.

The first Belfast steamboat was launched in 1820, but the shipyards' main development came after the harbour was modernised. 1853 saw the opening of the first big shipyard by Robert Hickson. He was soon bought out by Harland and Wolff, who built it into the largest in the world. Such a success encouraged other manufacturers to invest in industries in Belfast, and other towns in the vicinity began to share the fruits of its success.

This industrial revolution was to have a permanent effect on Irish history, because it separated the industrial north-east from the rest of the country.

In other areas of Ireland, agriculture still provided the raw materials for most industries, and where the factory system was established it was mainly as a method of processing farm products. Wexford produced farm machinery, brewing and distilling were centred in Dublin and Cork, Limerick and Dublin made confectionery, while creameries were set up throughout south Leinster and Munster.

Domestic industry declined as cheap, mass-produced goods from Britain flooded the market. At the same time, new agricultural technology meant that less hands were needed to work on farms. Many people left the land, moving to the cities in search of work, but few Irish towns or cities could provide enough jobs for them all. The ever-growing industries of Britain's north and midlands could, however, and the stream of emigration which began during the Famine continued right up to the mid-20th century.

The development of a nation-wide electricity network in Ireland was slow. Electricity was first introduced in the 1880s and by the 1920s there were hundreds of small generating stations throughout the country, supplying local needs.

But there were many areas — even some urban areas — which still had no electricity. The solution did not lie in building yet more stations, rather in setting up a network system, into which power would be fed and which would bring electricity to all areas within this network.

The Shannon Scheme at Ardnacrusha was a breakthrough. Not only was it the first big step in the setting-up of the network, not only was it massive in scale, but it used a plentiful and local energy source — moving water. In 1930 the first electricity produced there was fed into the network; Ardnacrusha was followed by other large stations — some hydro-electric, others using other fuels. They all generate electricity for the network in the Republic of Ireland, administered by the ESB, which was set up in 1927.

Nationwide electrification made an enormous difference to industry. It was no longer necessary for a factory to be built near its source of power; electricity could be brought almost anywhere. Industrial developments in Ireland between the 1920s and 1950s were largely made possible by the new electricity network. But it had other, equally important effects.

*Ardnacrusha on the Shannon.*

Many of the tasks of farming and housekeeping were lightened by electrically powered labour-saving devices, leaving people with more time to do other things in relation to both their work and leisure. Electricity also meant the rapid development of the new communication technology, which is the subject of a later section in this chapter. In short, the nationwide electricity network helped to narrow the gap between rural and urban living.

*'This improvin' of rural life is wonderful . . . Now the children'll be able to study till all hours of night for the Civil Service!' (Dublin Opinion's impression of the coming of electricity.)*

When the Irish Free State was set up in 1922, there were great hopes that Ireland would once again manufacture its own goods. The country was run efficiently, electricity supplies planned, but how could factories be established which could replace imported goods with Irish products? No answer came until 1932, when a new government decided to break up the free-trade area which existed between Britain and Ireland. Importers of British goods had to pay taxes; Irish manufacturers did not. Many factories were set up to make goods in Ireland. These were mostly factories which made the smaller things which are in daily use — sweets, buttons, bottles, cigarettes, toilet goods — rather than heavy industries, such as metal chemical, textile or engineering works. The machinery for the light industries was imported and set to work behind the tariff barrier.

This way of protecting Irish-made goods helped to build the industrial life of the country, particularly through the world-wide economic depression of the 1930s. By the 1950s, however, it had become clear that Irish industry would have to compete openly on the world market if it were to prosper, and the government of the day decided to abandon the policy of protection.

The decision to remove all barriers between Ireland and world markets was well-timed. It marked the start of a period of industrial growth, the Irish 'industrial revolution' of the 1960s.

# Transport

'A proof how little one-horse carriages wear roads, is the method used in Ireland to construct them; they throw up a foundation of earth in the middle of the space from the outsides, on that they immediately form a layer of limestone, broken to the size of a turkey's egg; on this a thin scattering of earth to bind the stones together, and over that a coat of gravel, where it

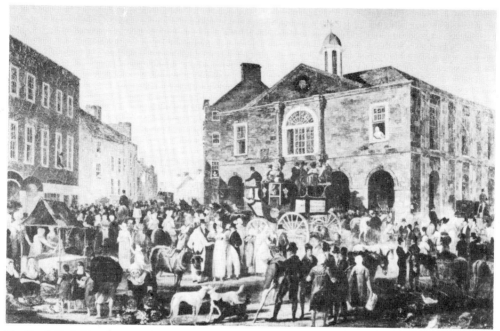

*The North Cork-Limerick stage coach in 1820.*

is to be had. Their carriages considered, no fault is to be found with this mode, for the road is beautiful and durable; but, being all finished at once, with very little or no time for settling, an English waggon would presently cut through the whole, and demolish the road as soon as made, yet it is perfectly durable under cars and coaches.'

Arthur Young: *Tour in Ireland, 1776-1779*

The great days of horse-drawn transport in Ireland came with the stage coach. These giant carriages carried up to 30 people and ran scheduled services on the main routes around the country. They began with short journeys from Dublin around 1730, but the most famous were the Post Office mail coaches which ran on main routes after 1790.

The stage coaches (and later, the railways which replaced them) only covered the main routes. Until the arrival of Charles Bianconi and his 'cars', there was no service for people who wanted to travel away from the main routes or for short distances.

When the young Bianconi came to Ireland from Italy in 1802, he travelled around Munster selling picture-frames and mirrors. This travelling job first gave him the idea of setting up a transport service *off* the main stage-coach routes.

From his first car, covering the 16 kilometres between Cahir and Clonmel in Tipperary in 1815, his service was a huge success and prospered right up to the coming of motor buses, long after his retirement in 1866.

There were reasons for his success. He used good strong horses, skilled drivers and well-built cars, which he designed himself. His service was reliable and as comfortable as was possible (passengers could pull on waterproof aprons when it was raining). Above all, Bianconi was a good business man. He based his service on what people needed, and did not try to compete with other public services. The coming of the railways did not mean his downfall. Quite the contrary, his cars now ran to and from railway stations to towns and villages off the rail routes. By 1860 Bianconi's cars ran over 6,400 kilometres every day.

*A Bianconi Car.*

## CANALS

Bianconi's type of transport was suited to a countryside dotted with market towns. However, it could not shift the large loads which would be needed by a factory. Land transport of heavy goods from Dublin to Galway took at least five days, and only small quantities could be moved. It was known that heavy goods could be moved more easily when floated on water. The main towns of Ireland were either coastal, or on navigable rivers. To extend the advantages of water transport, the engineers of the 18th century undertook the enormous task of building artificial inland waterways, canals, on which goods and passengers could be carried by horse-drawn barges.

The desire for a native supply of coal was the idea behind Ireland's first canal. Coal was being mined around Coalisland in Co. Tyrone, but it could not be moved to Dublin across country. In 1731 it was decided to build a canal linking Lough Neagh to Newry in Co. Down to Dublin. By this plan, coal was brought by water from Tyrone to Dublin, along the first true canal to be constructed in Britain or Ireland.

Sections of the rivers Lagan, Bann, Boyne, Barrow, Nore, Suir, Slaney and Shannon were also made navigable. By these means a whole new inland waterway network was created.

Passengers travelling to and from Dublin by canal faced many hours of travel. For example, the journey on the Grand Canal from Athy to Dublin in 1803 involved an overnight stay at Robertstown! Here is one traveller's account:

'Precisely as the clock struck one, the towing horse started, and we slipped through the water in the most delightful manner imaginable, at the rate of four miles an hour. The boat appeared to be about 35 feet long, having a raised cabin, its roof forming a deck to walk upon. The cabin was divided into a room for the principal passengers, having cushioned seats and windows in either side, and a long table in the middle, and into another room for the servants of the vessel and the pantry: the kitchen was in the steerage . . . The day was very fine, and the company very respectable and pleasant. We had an excellent dinner on board, consisting of a leg of boiled mutton, a turkey, ham, vegetables, porter, and a pint of wine each, at four shillings and ten pence a head . . . Our liquid road lay through very fine country, adorned with several noble seats . . . We slept at Robertstown, where there is a noble inn belonging to the Canal company, and before day-light set off for Dublin, where after descending a great number of locks, and passing through a long avenue of fine elms, we arrived about ten o'clock a.m. All the regulations of these boats are excellent. I was so delighted with my canal conveyance, that if the objects which I had in view had not been so powerful, I verily think I should have spent the rest of my time in Ireland in the Athy canal boat.'

Sir John Carr: *The Stranger in Ireland . . . in the year 1805*

Later, a 'fly-boat' service, involving three horses instead of one, speeded things up. The Dublin-Athy journey now only took seven hours.

But the full usefulness of the canals was never really put to the test. A far speedier way of moving both people and goods was already in existence even before the last canals were completed. The railways put an end to any hopes the canal-builders had of making inland waterways the main transport system in the country.

# CHEAP, SAFE, & EXPEDITIOUS TRAVELLING
## ROYAL CANAL PASSAGE BOATS

### DAY BOAT
Fly Boat to Mullingar
Every Morning at Nine o'clock

| FROM DUBLIN<br><br>TO MULLINGAR | Distance<br>in<br>miles | Hour of<br>Arrival<br>H   M | First<br>Cabin<br>s.   d. | Second<br>Cabin<br>s.   d. |
|---|---|---|---|---|
| Clonsilla | 8 | 10  30 | 0  10 | 0  7 |
| Rye Aqueduct  Leixlip | 11 | 10  55 | 1  3 | 0  10 |
| Maynooth | 15 | 11  25 | 1  6 | 1  0 |
| Kilcock | 19 | 12  0 | 2  0 | 1  3 |
| Ferns | 22 | 12  25 | 2  6 | 1  6 |
| Newcastle | 27 | 1  10 | 2  10 | 1  10 |
| Moyvalley | 31 | 1  40 | 3  3 | 2  2 |
| Boyne Aqueduct | 33 | 1  55 | 3  6 | 2  4 |
| Hill of Down | 36 | 2  15 | 3  9 | 2  6 |
| Thomastown | 42 | 2  55 | 4  4 | 2  10 |
| Down's Bridge | 47 | 3  55 | 4  10 | 3  3 |
| Mullingar | 52 | 4  30 | 5  6 | 3  6 |

### RATES OF ORDINARY

| *First Cabin* | s. | d. | *Second Cabin* | s. | d. |
|---|---|---|---|---|---|
| Breakfast with Eggs | 1 | 0 | Breakfast with an Egg | 0 | 10 |
| Luncheon | 0 | 8 | Dinner | 1 | 0 |
| Dinner | 1 | 8 | Porter per Bottle | 0 | 4 |
| Tumbler of Wine and Water | 0 | 6 | Guinness XX | 0 | 6 |
| Ditto of Brandy and Water | 0 | 10 | Ditto Pint | 0 | 3 |
| Ditto Whiskey and Water | 0 | 5 | Ale per Bottle | 0 | 6 |
| Porter per Bottle | 0 | 4 | Cider per Bottle | 0 | 8 |
| Guinness XX | 0 | 6 | Supper | 0 | 9 |
| Ditto Pint | 0 | 3 | Tea or Coffee after Dinner | 0 | 10 |
| Ale per Bottle | 0 | 6 | No Wine or Spirit to be sold in the Second | | |
| Cider per Bottle | 0 | 8 | Cabin. Children from Two to Ten Years old | | |
| Tea or Coffee after Dinner | 1 | 0 | to pay only Half Rate in each Cabin. | | |

### IRELAND'S CANALS

| *When Built* | *Name* | *Route* |
|---|---|---|
| 1731 | Newry Canal | Lough Neagh to Newry |
| 1784 | Lagan Navigation | Lough Neagh to Belfast |
| 1811 | Grand Canal | Dublin to River Shannon |
| 1817 | Royal Canal | Dublin to River Shannon |
| 1842 | Ulster Canal | Belfast to Lough Erne |
| 1859 | Ballinamore and<br>Ballyconnell Canal | Carried the Ulster Canal<br>to the Shannon |

Nevertheless, some freight continued to be moved on Irish canals right up to 1960.

## THE RAILWAY

Although the rotary steam engine designed by James Watt in 1781 revolutionised industry, it could not be used for transport because it was far too large to move. In 1805, however, another English engineer, Richard Trevithick, built a smaller engine with a higher steam pressure which was the first ever machine to move itself.

The first locomotives were used to move coal and iron in the mines and foundries. Otherwise, the new mode of transport did not have general use. It was only after George Stephenson built his famous 'Rocket' in the 1820s, that rail was seen as an efficient and safe way of travel. The steam locomotives were just the right kind of transport for Britain's new heavy industries — they had immense power, could travel at speeds unheard of before then, go wherever iron rails of the right gauge were laid. As a bonus, laying railway tracks was cheaper and easier than building canals.

By 1855 there were over 12,800 kilometres of railway tracks in Britain, largely built by workers who wandered from one job to another and who came to be known as 'navvies'. Many of these were Irishmen who emigrated during the Famine and the decades which followed it.

In 1834 a railway was laid from Dublin to Kingstown (Dun Laoghaire). Belfast was linked by a railway to Lisburn and Portadown in 1842, and most of the other important lines were completed by 1860, many of them taking the same routes as the old stage coaches once used.

*Railway builders in County Derry.*

## THE RAILWAY NETWORK

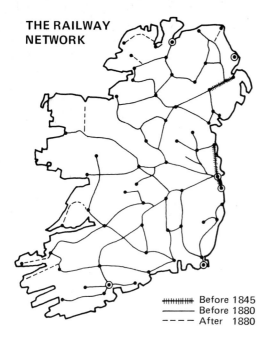

┼┼┼┼┼┼ Before 1845
───── Before 1880
- - - - After 1880

A town which had a railway station became more than ever a centre of life in the area. People travelled more, bringing prosperity to railway towns. Journeys were made for new purposes. Better-off people could take holidays at seaside centres like Youghal, Co. Cork, and later in the century when public holidays were introduced, poorer people went on day excursions to resorts such as Bray, Co. Wicklow. Railways encouraged tourism and also increased the speed with which goods were transported. In 1845 a load of coal took five days to get from Dublin to Galway by road and canal, but in 1853 a similar load took only ten hours by rail.

The railways also brought time-tables into the lives of the country people. A passing train marked the time of day, and for the first time it mattered that clocks in Galway told the same time as clocks in Dublin, Donegal or Wexford.

### THE COMING OF THE RAILWAY

Michael McGowan, returning to Derry from America in the late 19th century, is amazed at the changes he sees. He and his mates meet a man in a quayside pub, who tells them what has been happening while they were away:

'You don't have to walk to Cloghaneely this time", he said, 'as you and your fathers had to. The train goes now and you'll be able to take it as far as Cashelnagor.'

'It's good to hear that,' we all said together.

'And what's the reason for this sudden change?' I asked the gentleman.

'I'll tell you that,' he said, 'if you have time to listen to my story. A Board was set up called the Congested Districts Board and some years ago a man named Balfour visited your parts. He enquired about the condition of the people and when he had done that, he conferred with people in authority about schemes to help the poor districts that stretch from here westwards to the sea. As a result of that, the railway between Letterkenny and Burtonport was started.'

'It couldn't be that this work took very long,' said one of my friends.

'It didn't,' said the gentleman, 'and that's where the workers did themselves damage. They were so enthusiastic at the work that it only took two years to build the railway. Gangs of them all worked together and they tore hills away and filled in little valleys and it wasn't long until there was silence again all over the place. If they had had any sense, they could have made the work last much longer. And the pay they were getting wasn't even all that good — they were working from dawn to dusk for a half-crown a day.'

'What way did they bring the railway?' asked Hugh McGinley.

'They brought it out the very cheapest way for themselves,' said the gentleman, 'and they'll rue it for more than today. They built it as straight as they could over hills and dales and it doesn't go within miles of any village from here to Burtonport. If they had built it along the coast, as they should have done, the land would have been dear but instead they bought the cheaper land and built it around by the foot of the hills. Of course, from the tourists' point of view, it goes through some of the loveliest countryside in Ireland.'

'The fishermen of the Rosses have benefited by it,' said a man from Burtonport who was in our company.

'You could say that,' said the Derryman, 'and it will do this town good too. It has done so already. There's a man in this town that has made a small fortune out of clocks since the railway started — a man named Faller. He began making clocks and selling them for a pound each and there isn't a house between here and Arranmore that hasn't a clock now.' . . .

'Changes there are,' said the Derryman, 'and the people down by the sea where you live can be thankful to this new Board for many of them. They've done well for the fishing all around the coast; roads and bridges were built; grants were given to poor people to help them to build new houses; they're helping home industries and the weavers are very busy now making bawneen. There are twenty ways in which they're trying to help the people, late and all as it is. But better late than never.'

from: *The Hard Road to Klondyke*

Travelling in the early railways was not comfortable — unless one could afford to ride in the first-class covered compartments. The cheapest fares were in the third-class, open cars, exposed to wind, rain and soot from the locomotive. Breakdowns and delays were frequent. Nevertheless, the railways were the quickest and most reliable means of transport and were used by great numbers of people.

### MOTOR TRANSPORT

Both the canals and the railways had

*Making way for motor transport. A road gang in 1914 at work in County Mayo.*

one great problem — they provided an inflexible transport service. Bianconi's cars helped passengers travel to and from the canal and rail routes, but it was more difficult when it came to moving freight. As a result, industries and housing were located around canal harbours and rail heads.

New developments in transport were to have flexibility as their aim. In the 1890s a German engineer, Gottlieb Daimler, came up with the answer — a light carriage driven by a petrol-fuelled engine, a 'horseless carriage' which needed neither waterway nor rail to run on.

In 1914 the First World War began; the railways were taken over by the government and horses requisitioned for the army. During the war, petrol-driven trucks and buses became increasingly common. In 1918, when the army sold off its trucks and buses which had been used for war transport, they became available to private transport operators in towns all over Ireland. Motor transport took business from the railways, and put the horse-drawn cars off the road. In the 1920s bicycles were mass-produced cheaply enough for ordinary people to buy, and in a decade the transport system opened up and came more under personal control. People could work some distance from their homes, factories could be opened away from ports and railheads. In the cities a great movement of population away from the central city areas had already begun, and now there was little to hinder it. Many concepts which are part of modern towns and their development — for example, suburbs and residential areas, industrial zones, commuting to and from work — have been made possible by the flexibility of motor transport and the bicycle.

## CITY TRANSPORT

Up to now, this section has mainly dealt with transport between towns.

*Motoring in Glengarriff, County Cork. Motorists wore special clothing to protect themselves from wind, rain and flying mud.*

However, as cities grew, especially their suburbs, more and more people travelled *within* the urban area.

## IN THE HEART OF THE HIBERNIAN METROPOLIS

'Before Nelson's pillar trams slowed, shunted, changed trolley, started for Blackrock, Kingstown and Dalkey, Clonskea, Rathgar and Terenure, Palmerstown Park and Upper Rathmines, Sandymount Green, Rathmines, Ringsend and Sandymount Tower, Harold's Cross. The hoarse Dublin United Tramway Company's timekeeper bawled them off:

'Rathgar and Terenure!'
'Come on, Sandymount Green!'

Right and left parallel clanging ringing a double-decker and a single-deck moved from their railheads, swerved to the down line, glided parallel.

'Start, Palmerston Park!'

Under the porch of the general post office shoeblacks called and polished. Parked in North Prince's street His Majesty's vermilion mailcars, bearing on their sides the royal initials, E.R., received loudly flung sacks of letters, postcards, lettercards, parcels, insured and paid for, local, provincial, British and overseas delivery.

Grossbooted draymen rolled barrels dullthudding out of Prince's stores and bumped them up on the brewery float. On the brewery float bumped dullthudding barrels rolled by grossbooted draymen out of Prince's stores.'

James Joyce: *Ulysses*

By the 1870s enough people lived some miles from the city centres to make public-transport services possible. The first trams were horse-drawn, and ran on iron tracks set into the cobbled street. Later they were

*Dublin Tram — drawing by Frances Breen*

powered by electric lines overhead. Most areas of the city were on tram routes and few people had to walk very far to catch a tram. However, as the city grew, a more flexible service was needed, one which would serve the new areas that were being built. Slowly, motorised buses replaced the trams on the main routes.

## THE STATE AND PUBLIC TRANSPORT

When the Free State was founded in 1922, a large number of transport companies were in competition with each other, many losing money. The State set about bringing them together. In 1925 26 railway companies were joined to form the Great Southern Railway Company, which was to control all rail travel in Ireland.

The railways contnued to lose money and decline as road transport became more popular. Many road transport services were also brought under the GSR. It was hoped that there could be more control over public transport in general, and that money-losing services could be balanced by those making a profit. However, small private companies continued to provide services right up to the late 1930s, when all passenger services in the Free State came under the GSR or the Dublin United Tramway Company.

In 1944 these two companies merged to form Coras Iompair Eireann, a semi-State body with total control of all road and rail freight service. In 1950 CIE also took over the canals.

CIE has had a difficult task. It took over the maintenance of large networks of roads, railways and canals, too large for the population of this country. It cannot, like a private company, just provide services which will make money, but must see that all areas are served, even though it means a loss every year. It also faces a drop in the number of passengers in recent years as more and more people can afford to buy private cars.

In May 1936, another transport company was set up by the State — Aer Lingus, the national airline.

It was only after the Second World War that the airline started to expand. Its growth was helped by an agreement signed by the Irish and British Governments that Aer Lingus would be the only company to carry passengers between the two countries; in return, British airlines would own part of Aer Lingus. This agreement lasted until 1964, by which time Aer Lingus was strong enough not to need this kind of protection.

By the early 1960s Aer Lingus had, apart from its strong cross-channel service, a growing number of European routes and, most successful of all in financial terms, a transatlantic service using Boeings, the first of the high-speed jet aircraft.

*High Speed Surface Transit for the future, currently being developed by Japan Airlines.*

# Communications

In ancient Ireland, messages had to be carried from place to place in the memory of the messenger. Roman writing came with Christianity and the written word, on paper, meant that detailed communication and accurate reporting could now not only take place between people living far apart but even between people living in different times. The printing press, the 'mass production' of writing, increased the circulation of the written word, and therefore its power. Printed books, journals and pamphlets passed on ideas, news and messages.

Ireland's oldest existing newspaper, *The Limerick Chronicle,* was founded in 1776. Readers of newspapers in the 18th and early 19th century were those with education. However, during the 19th century, the number of people who could read grew, and in 1842 the weekly newspaper, *The Nation,* was founded by Thomas Davis, John Blake Dillon and Charles Gavan Duffy.

*The Nation* was a nationalist paper. Its editors wanted Irish people to be more aware of what being Irish meant, and so, as well as news, the paper also contained poems, stories and articles in Irish history. It was a success from its very first issue, and was widely read by all classes in Ireland. In many towns and villages people who could not read gathered together to hear the newspaper being read aloud.

Over the 19th century the majority of people came to understand the value of the skills of reading and writing. Not only could people read of far-off events in the newspapers, but they themselves could communicate with friends and relatives in distant places.

But everyone had to arrange and pay for the journey of their letters and parcels themselves. The first real sign of the new spirit of *mass* communication was the development of an organised postal service. A new post office, the General Post Office, was built in Dublin in 1815 to receive packets and letters to be carried on the stage coaches which travelled along the major roads of the country. In 1840 the post was re-organised. For a standard fee of one penny, the Post Office undertook to carry a letter anywhere in the United Kingdom. The fee was prepaid by fixing a stamp to the letter, which could then be dropped in any of the posting boxes placed on the streets by the Post Office. Office work was made easier, business speeded up, journeys and holidays more easily arranged, separated friends and families could easily keep in touch.

### THE TELEGRAPH:
### COMMUNICATION WITHOUT TRAVEL

However well organised the postal service, messages still took as long to reach their destination as it took to travel there. Even with the help of the railways, the post soon became too slow for the needs of industry and trade. The need for speed led Samuel Morse to invent a device which was simple but extraordinary in its effect. Morse devised a code which represented the letters of the alphabet by various combinations of long and short dashes. Messages translated into this code were flashed instantly and for great distances along electric wires. The transmitter tapped a button to send long and short impulses along the wire. At the receiving end, a pen was pressed against a moving roll of paper for the duration of each charge, and the message, which appeared on the paper as a series of dots and dashes, could be quickly decoded, and a reply sent if necessary. 'Tele-

# GENERAL PENNY POST-OFFICE.

*Comptroller*, Edward James Baynes, Esq.
*President and Chief Clerk*, Neal J. O'Neill, **Esq.**
*Collector*, William Barrington, Gentleman.

*In the City there are Six Collections and Deliveries daily, and in the Country two, Sundays excepted.*

| FOR THE CITY. | | FOR THE COUNTRY. | |
|---|---|---|---|
| 1st Dispatch | 8 o'Clock. | 1st Dispatch | 8 o'Clock. |
| 2d ditto | 10 ditto | 2d ditto | 2 ditto |
| 3d ditto | 12 ditto | | |
| 4th ditto | 2 ditto | | |
| 5th ditto | 4 ditto | | |
| 6th ditto | 6 ditto | | |

The Postage on each Letter, to and from all parts of the City, is one penny; beyond the City two-pence. The only place where letters can be post-paid is the General Post Office. No Letter exceeding four ounces will pass, except such as is intended for General or Foreign Dispatch.

## CITY RECEIVING HOUSES.

| | | | |
|---|---|---|---|
| Anne-street, south | 17 Digges-street | 14 Inns-quay | 16 Ormond-quay, upper |
| Baggot-street | 111 Dorset-street, upper | 75 James's-street | 38 Ormond-quay, lower |
| 65 Barrack-street | 4 Dorset-street, lower | 12 Kevin-street | 17 Pill-lane |
| 45 Bolton-street | 14 Echlin-lane | 6 Kildare-street | 1 Queen-street |
| 29 Bride-street | 3 Essex-bridge | 31 King-street, north | 77 Rogerson's-quay |
| 26 Bridge-street, lower | 30 Essex-street | 18 King-street, south | 23 Royal Arcade |
| 11 Brunswick-street | 141 Francis-street | 62 Leeson-street | Royal Hospital |
| 37 Camden-street | 24 George's-quay | 29 Manor-street | 115 Stephen's-green, west |
| 70 Capel-street, upper | 38 Golden-lane | 51 Mary-street | 18 Stephen's-street |
| 49 Capel-street | 104 Grafton-street | 21 Meath-street | 66 Summer-hill, upper |
| 163 Church street, old | 50 Great Britain-street | 133 Mecklenburgh-street | 1 Summer-hill, lower |
| 20 Clare-street | 85 Great Britain-street | 6 Merrion-row | 60 Thomas-street |
| 10 Cork-hill | Green-street | 9 Molesworth-street | 45 Townsend-street |
| 122 Cork-street | 1 Harcourt-street | 34 New-street | 4 Werburgh-street |
| Cross Poddle | 18 Holles-street | North Strand | |

Bags are made up, and despatched by the Belfast Morning Coach, which leaves Dublin at 7 A. M. and returns at 7 P. M. for

| Banbridge, | Castlebellingham, | Dromore, | Dunleer, | Lisburne and |
|---|---|---|---|---|
| Belfast, | Drogheda, | Dundalk, | Hillsborough, | Newry. |

\*\*\* Bags are also made up with British, Foreign, and State Letters, on Sundays, for all six day posts. The Cork Mail Coaches are dispatched as follows, one *by Clonmel*, at seven each evening, and the other *by Cashel*, at seven each morning.

All Double, Treble, and other Letters and Packets whatever, pay in proportion to the respective rates, of Single Letters. Packets chargable by Weight pay after the rate of four Single Letters for every ounce, and so in proportion for any greater weight, reckoning every quarter of an ounce equal to a Single Letter.

\*\*\*Members Franks are *chargeable* if above one ounce weight.

## RATES OF POSTAGES TO GREAT BRITAIN.

| | | *s.* | *d.* | | | *s.* | *d.* |
|---|---|---|---|---|---|---|---|
| Dublin and London | - - - - - - - | 1 | 3 | Waterford and London | - - - - - | 1 | 2 |
| Dublin and Holyhead | - - - - - - | 0 | 3 | Waterford and Milford | - - - - - | 0 | 2 |
| Dublin and Isle of Man | - - - - - | 1 | 7 | Donagadee and London | - - - - - | 1 | 4 |
| Dublin and Guernsey or Jersey | - - - - | 1 | 6 | Donagadee and Portpatrick | - - - | 0 | 2 |

## FOREIGN AND PACKET RATES OF POSTAGE FOR A SINGLE LETTER.

| | *s.* | *d.* | | | *s.* | *d.* |
|---|---|---|---|---|---|---|
| Dublin to France - - - - - - - | 2 | 3 | St. Helena - - - - - - - | 1 | 11½ |
| The Netherlands - - - - - - | 2 | 5 | Africa, except Cape of Good Hope, - - | 1 | 11½ |
| Germany, Switzerland, Turkey, Russia, Prussia, | | | MAILS MADE UP IN LONDON AS FOLLOWS | | | |
| Denmark, Sweden, and Norway - - | 2 | 9 | France, every Tuesday, Wednesday, Thursday, and | | |
| Italy, Turkey, through France - - - | 3 | 0 | Friday. | | |
| Spain, through France - - - - - | 3 | 3 | Holland and Netherlands, Germany and North of | | |
| Portugal - - - - - - - - | 2 | 11 | Europe, every Tuesday and Friday. | | |
| Madeira - - - - - - - - | 3 | 0 | Jamaica and America, first Wednesday monthly. | | |
| Brazils - - - - - - - - | 3 | 11 | Leeward Islands, first and third Wednesday monthly. | | |
| Gibraltar - - - - - - - - | 3 | 3 | Madeira and Brazils first Tuesday monthly. | | |
| Malta, Corfu, and Mediterranean - - | 3 | 7 | Portugal, weekly, Tuesdays. | | |
| West Indies - - - - - - - | 2 | 7 | Gibraltar, Malta, Corfu and Mediterranean first | | |
| America - - - - - - - - | 2 | 7 | Tuesday monthly. | | |
| New South Wales - - - - - - | 1 | 11½ | | | |

*Postage rates, 1829.*

communications', that is, instant communication over long distance, had come into being.

By 1858 a transatlantic cable linked Ireland and Britain with America. The telegraph could make enquiries on deliveries or prices, check time-tables, send urgent messages, avoid delay and misunderstanding in a thousand ways. Most important, reports of happenings in one place could be sent immediately around the country and across the world.

The telegraph was fast, but messages had to be sent through an office and a trained operator. In 1876 Alexander Bell invented a machine which enabled the human voice to be carried along an electric wire. The caller spoke into a microphone which vibrated and transmitted a fluctuating current, recreating the sound waves which had entered the microphone.

The telephone, as it was called, was easily installed, even in the home. A central exchange would connect callers with any number they required, causing a bell in the receiver's telephone to ring, attracting the attention of anyone near it. It was a magnificent invention. The first exchange in Ireland was built in 1880, but some parts of the country waited many years for a local exchange to be installed.

The telephone did not end the rush of discoveries and inventions in the field of telecommunications. Radio waves, travelling freely through the atmosphere, were explored. In 1902 Guglielimo Marconi, an Italian engineer, opened a station in Clifden, Co. Galway, which could transmit radio signals across the Atlantic without using wires at all. The 'wireless' message could be heard by any-

*The shore end of the Atlantic telegraph cable is laid at Valentia Island from the steamer 'William Corry'.*

*The mail coaches depart from the G.P.O., amidst great consternation.*

*The Volta Cinema in Mary Street, Dublin's first cinema, was managed briefly in 1909-10 by James Joyce.*

one with a receiver within range.

Why not everyone? The idea of broadcasting, that is, sending general messages to anyone who might be listening, followed shortly. The whole country could listen to news, interviews, commentaries, reports and entertainments carried into the home by radio waves broadcast to the nation.

In 1925 a radio station, 2RN (later to become Radio Eireann), began to broadcast programmes from Dublin. The excitement of events such as All-Ireland Finals gathered people around wireless sets from Antrim to Cork. One talking-point could fire the imagination of the country, making national events real and important.

### PICTURES OF THE CHANGING WORLD

The discovery of ways of reproducing images was the next big step in the communications 'revolution'. As early as the 1830s, Frenchmen Joseph Niepce and his partner Louis Daguerre had worked out that if a light-sensitive surface were exposed for a controlled length of time, an image would be left on that surface. Later, a way of printing the image onto special paper was developed, producing what was to be known as a 'photograph'.

In 1847 the Irish Famine was reported by newspapers around the world, and artists were sent to Ireland to make drawings which would illustrate the reports. If the Famine had happened ten years later, there would have been photographs of the terrible scenes. The American Civil War of 1862-65 was photographed by the first press photographers, and from that time the image framed by the photographer in his lens has been every person's image of what happened.

At the beginning of the new century experimenters began using light to project images from film onto a screen. They found that when image followed image faster than the eye could detect, the characters appeared to come to life on the screen. It was 'the wonder of the age'.

With the development of sound

*Eamonn De Valera broadcasting to the nation.*

recording, by the late 1920s events (both real and fictional) could now be presented to the public in both picture and sound, in a way which was more vivid and immediate than the written word. At the same time, however, people had to go to cinemas to see the moving pictures. Radio and the newspapers, on the other hand, brought the outside world into people's homes. In 1926 John Logie Baird discovered that pictures as well as sound could be broadcast in the form of waves. His new invention combined the vividness of the cinema with the intimacy of the radio. It was called television. In 1936 the British Broadcasting Corporation introduced the first public television service.

*Marconi with an early radio set.*

# The Urban Way of Life

For the people living in towns and cities in the first decades of this century, life had already been transformed by the developments of the previous hundred years. Electricity generators supplied power for trams and lighting; messages were being relayed across the Atlantic by wireless. Cars with petrol-driven engines were on the streets. Cinemas advertised moving picture shows. The flight of the Wright Brothers made air travel a reality.

But the change went deeper than new machines or the factory way of production. A new way of life had emerged. The traditional society was being replaced by one which was constantly seeking a faster and more efficient way of doing things.

This new, urban way of life would have seemed 'foreign' to people living in the country; in Ireland the majority of the people still lived in rural areas. In towns and cities new generations were growing up for whom noise, traffic, smoke and factories were more real than fields and farm, and for whom the slow, unchanging life of the countryside would have been baffling.

### A COUNTRYMAN COMES TO THE CITY

'I felt a prod in my shoulder. 'The bus is coming,' said George.

She comes across with a loud grating noise. The crowd moves towards her, myself and my companion among them. She moves away rapidly. Soon motors and cars of all sorts are passing each other like ants, the bus turning the corners like the wind and a tumult in my head from the horns blowing to let others know they are coming. Isn't it great the intelligence of the drivers to guard

*Adam's Court, Dublin, 19th century.*

themselves against one another! For myself, I did not know any moment but I would be splintered.

We reached O'Connell Bridge and got out. Trams and motors roaring and grating, newspaper-sellers at every corner shouting in the height of their heads, hundreds of people passing this way and that without stopping, and every one of them, men and women, handsomely got up.

The trouble now was to cross the street. A man would make the attempt, then another, an eye up and an eye down, a step forward and a step back, until they would reach the other side.

'Oh Lord, George, this is worse than to be back off the quay of the Blasket waiting for a calm moment to run in.'

He laughed. 'Here is a calm moment now,' he said suddenly. Off we went in a flutter, George gripping my arm, now forwards, now backwards, until we landed on the opposite side.'

Maurice O'Sullivan: *Twenty Years A-Growing*

*Busy city scene showing a great variety of transport and dress. King Street, Cork around the turn of the century.*

Although city people might have thought that the country stayed the same as the city changed, this was not the case. Rural industry had declined, the population had grown smaller and the influence of the city began to be felt throughout the country, even in the more remote areas.

The city was taking away the ability of a town to supply its own needs or to employ the children who grew up in it. Food was still produced there, but clothes, tools, furnishing items — those things which used to express the tradition and character of a society — were factory products from the city. National education had taught people to read and speak English which, for many, was the language of the big world beyond the parish.

Older people felt that their world was passing away. In many ways, they were right. The city was the part of society most ready to change; it was to touch everything and give it an urban character.

### THE ROCKY ROAD TO DUBLIN

In Dublin next arrived,
I thought it such a pity
To be so soon deprived
A view of that fine city.
Then I took a stroll
All among the local quality
My bundle it was stole
In a neat locality.
Something crossed my mind
Then I looked behind
No bundle could I find
Upon my stick a-wobblin,
Inquiring for the rogue
They said my Connacht brogue
Wasn't much in vogue
On the rocky road to Dublin,

Whack-fol-de-rol . . .

*Saturday market-day bustle and business at the Coal Quay, Cork, c.1881.*

*Part Four*
# URBAN LIFE TODAY

# Ireland Before the 1960s

'If you went up the North Circular as far as the Big Tree Belfast was on the first turn to the right. Straight ahead. I knew that when I was seven. The country lay out there. I visited it with my grandmother one day she and Lizzie MacKay went out for a breath of air.

After dinner on a Sunday she put on her black coat and hat and a veil with little black diamonds on it and off we went. We went up the canal from Jones Road Bridge to Binn's Bridge (and that was nearly in the country already) and into Leech's.

There we sat having a couple till it was shutting and time to get the tram into the real country.

Lizzie and she got a dozen of large bottles and the loan of a basket and we got a currant pan and a half pound of cooked ham in the shop next door and got on the tram for Whitehall.

'I see yous are well-heeled,' says the conductor, looking at the basket.

'Well, the country, sir,' says my grandmother. 'You'd eat the side wall of a house after it.'

'You're going all the way?'

'To the very end,' says Lizzie MacKay. 'All the way to Whitehall.'

'And I don't suppose that'll be the country much longer,' says the conductor. 'There's houses everywhere now. Out beyond Phibsboro church. They're nearly out to where Lord Norbury disappeared on the way home and the coachman only felt the coach getting lighter on the journey and when he got to the house your man was disappeared and the devil was after claiming him, and good enough for him after the abuse he gave poor Emmet in the dock.'

My grandmother and Lizzie MacKay bowed their heads and muttered, 'Amen.'

'They're nearly out to there,' said the conductor, 'and it won't be long before they're at Whitehall,' giving the bell a bang to hurry the driver up before the builders got there.'

Brendan Behan: *After The Wake*

## POPULATION CHANGE IRELAND 1926 - PRESENT

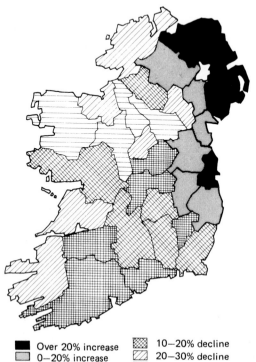

- ■ Over 20% increase
- □ 0–20% increase
- ▦ 0–10% decline
- ▨ 10–20% decline
- ▧ 20–30% decline
- ▤ Over 30% decline

---

A HUMAN SCALE

---

In 1950 life in Ireland was not all that different from 1900. The cities were seen as different and distinct from the country. People came to Dublin and Cork for jobs, or to shop for things which were not available elsewhere.

## ENTERING THE CITY

The city lies ahead. The vale
is cluttering as the train speeds through.
Hacked woods fall back; the scoop and swell
of cooling towers swing into view.

Acres of clinker, slag-heaps, roads
where lorries rev and tip all night,
railway sidings, broken sheds,
brutally bare in arc-light.

summon me to a present far
from Pericles's Athens, Caesar's Rome.
to follow again the river's scar
squirming beneath detergent foam.

I close the book, and rub the glass;
a glance ambiguously dark
entertains briefly scrap-yards, rows
of houses, and a treeless park.

like passing thoughts. Across my head
sundry familiar and strange
denizens of the city tread
vistas I would, and would not, change.

Birth-place and home! The diesels' whine
flattens. Excited and defiled
once more, I heave the window down
and thrust my head out like a child.

*Tony Connor*

## CHANGING POPULATION PATTERNS

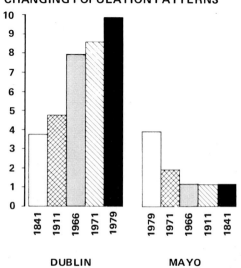

## IRELAND'S POPULATION MOVES TO CITIES

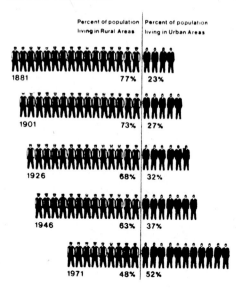

*In the 19th century most of Ireland's people lived in the country. Since 1971, however, the majority live in urban areas.*

They came to see 'the fashions', to examine hardware shops, to visit the Spring Show at the RDS, to visit relations or friends, or to attend weddings.

And the cities themselves had the slightly musty character of large country towns. They had a very particular atmosphere, a 'shabby gentility' it has been called. The old buildings still stood, and the towns, although dull, had a human scale.

There was not much money around, and it was carefully spent. People recalling their lives before the 1960s usually tell of thriftiness and care. Not everybody could afford butter or marmalade for their bread. Meat was often a luxury. Coats were carefully bought and handed on until they fell apart. Shoes were bought for their strength of character; trousers, shirts and jumpers could look forward to long and useful careers, passing from one member of a family to the next. Cars and bicycles were seen as long-term investments, and received the necessary care.

*Dutch homes gutted after World War II.*

Owning a house was a lifetime commitment for those who had steady jobs, and an impossible dream for many. Building estates were not enormous, and tended to reflect the quiet conservatism of the time.

There were many reasons for this austerity. Ireland was not a rich country. It had a small population which was declining in numbers. Most of the population loss was through emigration, as there were not enough jobs to be filled. The country had no huge manufacturing centres such as existed in Britain. The only exception to this rule was around Belfast, and the population of Northern Ireland actually increased between 1926 and 1966.

The belief in national poverty ran deep. Even the school books taught that Ireland had no industrial resources. It was not until the 1960s that the true extent of Ireland's mineral and fuel wealth came to be appreciated. Moreover, between 1920 and 1960, many of the Irish people were still licking the wounds inflicted in the war of independence and the civil war which followed it.

However, life in Europe and much of America was not all that different. The world was recovering from a variety of man-made disasters in the 20th century, the First World War, the Great Depression of the 1930s, and the Second World War. The recovery from these traumas was slow, but when it came, it was astounding.

### CHANGE IN THE POST-WAR WORLD

The Second World War ended in Europe and Asia in 1945. It left over 15 million people dead, and countless wounded. Large areas of Japan had been devastated by the only atomic weapons ever used against civilian targets. Elsewhere in the world, but especially in Europe, cities had been levelled by bombing, artillery and streetfighting. Families and friendships had been scattered, homes destroyed. Huge amounts of wealth and production capacity had been devoted to winning the war, and when the production of war materials stopped, on top of the return of hundreds of thousands of soldiers from the front, there was widespread unemployment and dislocation. After the turmoil and barbarity of the preceding six years, most people were content to enjoy peace and to pick up the scattered fragments of their lives.

Gradually, in the 1950s, prosperity returned. Employment grew in the United States and western Europe, industry returned to peace-time production as a demand rose. Factories that had been adapted to the production of tanks and armoured cars returned to the assembly of motor cars. Similarly, other plants turned from uniforms to overcoats. While austerity had been the keynote in the post-war period, new styles began to emerge as people found they had money to spare after buying essential goods.

This growing prosperity brought a great increase in the manufacture of light consumer goods, such as electrical appliances, drugs, cosmetics, magazines, motor accessories, clothes and later, transistor radios and televisions. However, the work involved in making these goods was often boring and repetitive, and workers in the wealthier nations found it unattractive. In some countries, such as Great Britain, it was done by immigrants, but many of the manufacturers looked outside their own countries

*Sean Lemass addressing the United Nations in 1963.*

for sites for their factories. Some companies formed large corporations which could plan production for the world market. Known as *multinationals,* they shifted their operations from country to country looking for the lowest production costs they could find.

### ECONOMIC CHANGE IN IRELAND

In all of these developments there were opportunities for Ireland, which had a large, cheap labour force. In 1958 the government published a Programme for Economic Expansion. Foreign businesses were encouraged to come to Ireland with promises of massive tax concessions, large construction grants and cheap labour costs.

In 1959 Sean Lemass became Taoiseach and introduced a new style of politics. He looked outwards for opportunities in the drive to turn Ireland into a modern industrialised nation. For this to happen, Irish factories needed to be able to sell their goods abroad at competitive

*Shannon Industrial Estate and New Town.*

prices. In 1965 Lemass lifted the heavy tax imposed on imported goods and signed a Free Trade Agreement with Great Britain. Ireland applied to join the EEC, the European Economic Community, and accepted the fact that their industry would have to face foreign competition.

The new policy came at just the right time. The market for consumer goods expanded dramatically in the boom period of the 1960s as the large number of children born in the years after the war reached their teens and became consumers. The success of the new policy of Lemass was evident — the census of 1966 showed that the population of Ireland was rising again, for the first time since the Famine.

Many of the new jobs that were being found were outside the major cities, because factories were now powered by electricity, and did not need to be near traditional sources of energy. Almost all, however, grouped workers together, either in traditional urban areas such as the growing suburbs of Dublin, Cork, Galway and Belfast, or in new urban centres like Shannon. One way or another,

the people who filled the new industrial jobs, wherever they themselves came from, began to share the international urban lifestyle that was further and further removed from the lifestyle their parents and grandparents had known, and that grew ever closer to the lifestyle of big cities everywhere.

CYNDDYLAN ON A TRACTOR

Ah, you should see Cynddylan on a tractor,
Gone the old look that yoked him to the soil;
He's a new man now, part of the machine,
His nerves of metal and his blood oil.
The clutch curses, but the gears obey
His least bidding, and lo, he's away
Out of the farmyard, scattering hens.
Riding to work now as a great man should,
He is the knight at arms breaking the fields'
Mirror of silence, emptying the wood
Of foxes and squirrels and bright jays.
The sun comes over the tall trees
Kindling all the hedges, but not for him
Who runs his engine on a different fuel.
And all the birds are singing, bills wide in vain,
As Cynddylan passes proudly up the lane.

*R. S. Thomas*

# After 1960: The New Urban Lifestyle

The 1960s was a decade of rebellion and upheaval, as the post-war generation challenged the ideas of the previous one, demanding peace and honesty, as well as commitment to social justice, freedom and equality of sex, race and creed.

### NEW IDEAS

It was a time when people began to look at the accepted values of their own society with new eyes. The traditional roles of men and women, the family, young people and educators were questioned. Attitudes began to change, but slowly, and many of the questions asked then are still debated hotly in Ireland today, 20 years later.

With the growing prosperity and freedom of the sixties, people began to look beyond their own society, and its problems to the world as a whole. Among the ideas which emerged was the realisation that the human race was violently abusing the earth it depended upon, that pollution endangered the existence of all living things, that rich nations spent billions of dollars on weapons while poor nations starved, and that the earth's resources were limited; in short, that everyone's survival depended on co-operation. Most importantly, people realised that they did not have to accept the way things are, that protest and argument can change the course of history.

In religion, the second Vatican Council led to sweeping changes in the way the Catholic religion was practised. This was bound to have a huge impact in Ireland, where Catholicism was practised with

*Protesting students in the late 1960s.*

unusual strictness. The Church's teaching shaped people's lives, government policies on many issues were clearly influenced by the bishops, and education was firmly organised along religious lines.

After the Vatican Council some people brought up in old Irish Catholicism found the new liberal and forgiving Church of the 1960s difficult to accept, but in general the change-over to modern Catholicism went remarkably smoothly in Ireland. A new openness could be seen, as well as a new concern for social justice. Ireland, which until the 1960s had been an inward-looking and cautious country, now began to look out into the world without fear.

## TELECOMMUNICATIONS

Apart from the growing affluence in the '60s and early '70s, the single most important factor in the spread of the modern urban lifestyle in Ireland was the communications revolution of the 20th century. From the first emigrant letters that arrived back from Britain and America in the 19th century to the latest satellite transmissions on television, communications systems have carried the same basic message to countless Irish homes, *the big city life is bright and attractive and pays well.*

By New Year's Eve in 1961, when RTE television began broadcasting, many Irish people were already familiar, through films, magazines and radio, with the glittering world beyond their shores, although they did not see themselves as part of it. This began to change in the 1960s as the influence of the mass media, especially television, grew. The television set brought a vast store of carefully packaged information and entertainment into the home, at the touch of a button.

*The world's press photograph a gunman in Belfast. Photographs of this kind help to sell newspapers and the presence of the press certainly encourages flamboyant displays of political extremism.*

Television is an extraordinary medium. It brings us closer to great events all over the world, which can be watched as they happen. An attempt to assassinate the American President can be seen within hours of the act. The World Cup and Olympic Finals can be watched 'live'. People worry about the fate of aeroplane passengers trapped by hijackers in Tripoli. Just as the television brings the world to Ireland, it also brings Ireland to the world. Violence as well as sports and cultural events have all been broadcast from this country.

However, television can also distort the line between fact and fiction. In 1980 85,000,000 Americans, the largest audience in the USA ever, watched an episode of the soap opera 'Dallas', to find out who had shot one of the leading characters. When the truth was revealed, it made international headlines as *news*. On the other hand, some observers maintain that at the time of the real-life shooting of US President, Ronald Reagan, many people were unable to distinguish between it and fictional violence on TV.

The ability of television to influence attitudes worries many people. Is the lifestyle shown in imported programmes very different to ours? The characters often seem to have casual attitudes towards sex, violence and crime, for example. There is no doubt that they are highly entertaining, but some people think a lot of programmes have little to do with life in Ireland.

At the same time, many people *want* imported programmes. During the 1970s a massive campaign was launched in the parts of Ireland only reached by RTE for more channels to be broadcast. In response to this, RTE 2 was launched in 1977. It selects most of its programmes from other TV stations and rebroadcasts them. In many ways its output defines Ireland as a province of Britain, and to a lesser degree, of America. Programmes like 'Top of the Pops', broadcast on RTE 2, introduces all the latest fashions in music and clothes in Britain to Ireland; 'Match of the Day' makes Irish viewers expert on the workings of the Football League in Britain.

As time goes on and more television channels become available, this

## LICENSED TV SETS IN THE IRISH REPUBLIC

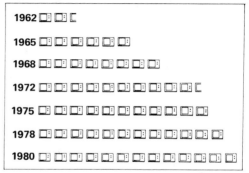

Each ⬜ represents 50,000 sets. NB. These figures are based on the number of TV licences issued each year; the actual number of TV sets would be considerably higher. (Source: Dept. of Posts and Telegraphs)

trend will accelerate.

The modern mass media, especially television, have made everyone part of a global village, or to be more exact, a global urban community. They are of ever-increasing importance in our lives. They channel our information and entertainment. They influence our attitudes and beliefs. How will we cope with them in the future? Do we need to teach children how to 'read' television as we teach them how to 'read' books? If television is to serve us well, then we must control it. It is, after all, only a medium of communication. As such it is only as good or as bad as the use we make of it.

"Bhí fear ann fadó agus fadó a bhí — will ye listen to me?" (Dublin Opinion)

FOR THE
GIRL
WHO DOESN'T
HAVE TO
PROVE
A THING.

## THE CONSUMER SOCIETY

The ideal consumer is a person with money to spare who would rather spend than save, and who is open to suggestion about what to buy. Irish people in the 1930s were not good consumers, even when they had money to spare, which was not often. They were cautious, since money was hard to come by. They cared for simple, hard-wearing things which served them well. Manufacturers stressed how useful and economic their products were.

Modern advertising sometimes mentions these qualities, especially since the recession of the 1970s, but more often it works in a very different way. 'Our product is fun', the ads suggest, 'and part of a beautiful and successful world. If you buy our product, *you* will share in that world.'

During the 1970s an interesting change took place in the mass media in America. Many long-established newspapers collapsed to be gradually replaced by more specialist magazines and journals. A similar change began in television in 1977, when viewing figures began to decline.

The term 'mass-media' is becoming less accurate. Viewers will soon be able to choose which programmes they want to watch, and when. Satellites will link thousands of stations around the earth, allowing us to choose to watch Russian melodramas or Japanese athletics, if we wish.

Apart from satellites, the most important breakthrough in communications is the development of fibre-optics, tiny threads of the world's purest glass carrying 50 million telephone calls each; the copper wires of our present system carry only 32. These cables can also carry computer data, information services and television signals.

When cable TV systems are generally established, it will be possible for anyone to make and sell programmes, provided they can organise and pay for them. Once completed, the programme will be recorded in a computerised catalogue. The viewer will dial the programme's index number, and the authors and participants will be paid from the royalties earned.

This technology will change the nature of television as we know it. Many programmes will never be broadcast by national stations like BBC and RTE, but will simply be made available to

Elvis Presley, one of the most important popular entertainers ever. Yet, in his early days most adults saw him as an indecent, overgrown teenager.

cable systems. We will have reached a point where we will have an endless supply of television programmes. Our only remaining problem will be *how* to choose our viewing!

### YOUNG PEOPLE AS CONSUMERS

In 1980, the average weekly expenditure of single people between the ages of 10 and 24 in the Republic of Ireland was £11.50 per head.

That is a total of nearly £9.75 million *each week*.

How was it spent?

| | |
|---|---|
| Clothes/shoes | 22% |
| Drinks (alcoholic + soft drinks) | 12% |
| Cinema/theatre/dancing | 11% |
| Gifts | 10% |
| Fares/travelling | 7% |
| Sweets/confectionery | 7% |
| Meals out | 7% |
| Cigarettes/tobacco | 6% |
| Other items | 18% |

*Source: Irish Marketing Surveys*

In most countries in the world, young people are expected to respect and listen to their elders. The adult world often tends to treat teenage experiences as unimportant. In the 1950s this began to change dramatically, especially in America, where one of the most affluent societies ever known was emerging. Films and pop music began to reflect the situations and feelings of teenagers. Many young Americans were listening to black rhythm 'n' blues radio stations and country music stations. In the middle '50s these elements fused in an explosion called rock 'n' roll.

Over the generation that followed, there were many changes of style and direction in pop music. By the time Elvis Presley died in 1977 at the age of 41, the world had come to accept pop music and to understand that even rebels mature. Rock 'n' roll and its many offshoots are now seen as one of the most important forms of modern music, full of invention and excitement. It is difficult to imagine anything that could describe the world we live in more vividly.

A measure of the vast power of the youth market in Ireland came in 1978 when RTE launched a special channel to cater for young people. 'Radio Two' is modelled on commercial pop music stations around the world. Its disc-jockeys sound bubbly and vaguely American, and many of the advertisements it carries are for international youth products, Coca-Cola, jeans, clothes, junk-food and cosmetics. This international youth culture is one of the most powerful forces for spreading the urban message in Ireland. All over the country, the same clothes are worn by young people and the same music heard. By the late 1970s it had become impossible to distinguish an Athlone teenager from a Liverpool teenager by appearance or taste.

# A Gathering Storm

The Irish are not alone in their attraction to the modern urban way of life. All over the world the demand is the same. People have seen the consumer society, and they like it. In material terms, the people of Ireland have never had it so good. At the same time, even the biggest, richest and most glamorous cities in the developed world are encountering other aspects of the modern urban lifestyle that are less attractive.

Urban violence is a growing threat to city life. So, too, is pollution, from industrial plants as well as the exhaust fumes of cars. Housing and employment are other problems, as cities become refuges for homeless and workless millions. The astonishing

*Youths photographed in Dublin. However, there is nothing about their appearance that tells where they are from. They could be from anywhere in Ireland or Britain.*

new technology of the computer and the microchip offers mankind the possibility of a brave new world, without drudgery, on the one hand, but also holds the possibility of vast upheaval in our work and attitudes to it. This, and the seemingly eternal reshaping of the city streets by new buildings, offer one of the most potent challenges to urban dwellers: the problem of change itself. This part of the book takes a look at some of the problems facing the modern city dweller.

## TRANSPORT

The years since 1960 have seen major changes in Ireland's transport system. A generation of growing urbanisation has outdated some methods of transport and fostered others. The growing population has brought new demands and new problems, as old roads and streets try to cope with the scourge of traffic. Even the most remote areas have been touched.

The massive growth in the traffic on Irish roads is closely connected with the spread of urban life. People have more money to spend on cars; more and more people live a lifestyle which is dependent on having a car; commuters drive to and from work daily, usually one person to a car. As affluence increases, people do not hesitate to drive some distance to buy luxury goods or be entertained.

New factories are mainly located on industrial estates, and have been built near large population centres, often far from port and rail services. As a result, trucks are used to transport the raw materials and to distribute the finished products. Heavy freight nowadays is packed in containers built to fit ships, trains and the giant trucks known as juggernauts.

A tourist came in from Orbitville,
parked in the air, and said:

The creatures of this star
are made of metal and glass.

Through the transparent parts
You can see their guts.

Their feet are round and roll
on diagrams or long

measuring tapes, dark
with the white lines.

They have four eyes.
The two in back are red.

Sometimes you can see a five-eyed
one, with a red eye turning

on the top of his head
He must be special —

the others respect him
and go slow

when he passes, winding
among them from behind.

They all hiss as they glide,
like inches, down the marked

tapes. Those soft shapes,
shadowy inside

the hard bodies — are they
their guts or their brains?

*May Swenson*

*'I see the Maguire boys are home for Christmas'.*

'There's no doubt about it, Cassidy's going all out to support the Tourist Board's policy of giving American visitors American hotel conditions!' (Dublin Opinion)

NEW CARS PURCHASED IN THE REPUBLIC OF IRELAND 1960-80

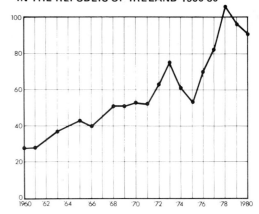

These figures are based on first registrations for each year. The decline in 1974-75 was a result of the oil crisis of 1973-74. The abolition of road-tax in 1977 led to a large increase in car sales.

Source: Central Statistics Office

A traffic jam after the opening of the new Matt Talbot Bridge in Dublin.

The public transport system has found it very difficult to provide an adequate service. Heavy traffic impedes buses; many new housing areas are not properly served; railways, built over a century ago, are not near many modern industrial and residential zones; travellers are not always ready to tailor their plans to suit timetables.

The result of this volume of traffic in Irish towns is frequent chaos:

*O'Connell Street, Limerick.*

- Cities are choked with traffic, in the morning and evening rush hours; some streets are practically impassable all day.
- Huge trucks cause vibrations which unsettle the foundations and brickwork of older buildings.
- Narrow, winding streets are 'bottlenecks' for through traffic.
- Villages, towns and suburban areas are unsafe and noisy to live in.

- Urban bus services cannot keep to their schedules because streets are jammed.
- Road surfaces quickly crumble under heavy traffic and have to be repaired. Road works cause more traffic congestion.

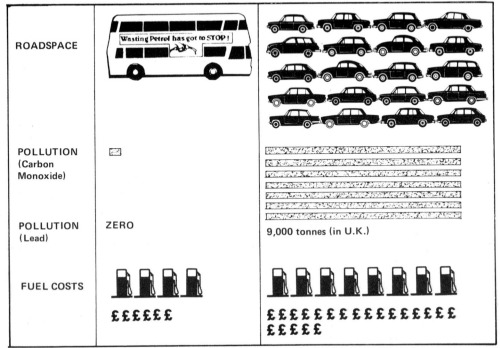

| | | |
|---|---|---|
| **ROADSPACE** | | |
| **POLLUTION** (Carbon Monoxide) | | |
| **POLLUTION** (Lead) | ZERO | 9,000 tonnes (in U.K.) |
| **FUEL COSTS** | £££££ | ££££££££££££££ ££££ |

*If public transport is fully used, it is far more economical and less polluting than private transport. However, an empty bus is more wasteful than a car; and many people also find buses far less comfortable and convenient.*

The aim of any plan must be to ease the flow of traffic through town and countryside. At the same time, people and goods must be able to move with ease wherever required.

Solution:
## BETTER ROADS?
*How?*

- Improve the road network throughout the country by widening major roads into multi-lane freeways and by building by-passes around towns and villages.
- Develop the urban road system by building an outer ring road, to enable traffic to avoid the city altogether; a multi-lane road encircling the inner city, to allow traffic to move more rapidly around the business and commercial centre; large multi-purpose roads in the suburbs to link the outer and inner ring roads; and multi-storey car-parking facilities at exit points from the inner ring route into the city.

**Problems**

- Roadbuilding is very expensive, and maintenance would put an enormous burden on local ratepayers.
- Improved road networks are likely to attract yet more traffic into the system.
- Motorways disrupt life; they separate communities which have developed over generations.
- Areas of open country, already disappearing as towns grow, would have to be sacrificed for road-building.
- In urban areas, motorways destroy the cityscape. Areas along the route are let run down as land is bought up.
- Houses and historic buildings have to be demolished.
- Attempts to build by-passes around towns or suburban centres are often opposed by powerful local interests, who believe that business will be diverted away from the town.

Solution:
## BETTER PUBLIC TRANSPORT?
*How?*

- Transfer heavy freight to the railways.
- Develop the urban public transport system by extending the overground rail network around the city, and building underground lines linking inner-city areas; increasing the number of special road lanes for buses; and reducing all-day parking in the city, even forbidding private cars in the city at certain times of the day.

**Problems**

- The rail network is not suitable for modern freight, as many of the ports which handle container traffic have no rail links.
- Up to now, urban public transport has proved time-wasting, inflexible and not suited to people's needs.
- Many services, for example, only provide transport from suburban areas into the city centre and not from one area to another on the same side of the city. People associate public transport with long, uncomfortable journeys. Any new system would have to be radically improved before winning the trust of the public.
- The increasing number of strikes which affect present public transport systems would cause even more disruption if private cars were no longer accommodated in inner-city areas.

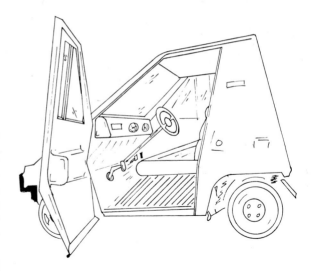

This is the Comuta-car which was introduced to the Irish market in 1981. It is powered by batteries that are recharged at night. Its costs are estimated at 1.3 pence per mile. Even if new sources of oil are found in the future, and natural fuels such as hydrogen and methane are developed, small pollution-free cars like this one are likely to be a popular form of private transport for future city-dwellers.

New theories being developed in the United States have suggested that the trains could be the major long-distance transport system of the future. The idea is simple but revolutionary.

Huge tunnels would be dug with lasers miles underground. Ultra-high speed trains would travel across and between continents at 5 − 6,500 kilometres per hour.

*Designed by Pininfarina of Turin, this C.N.R. aerodynamic car may be a feature of the future.*

## HOUSING

One of the most important tasks that the Irish governments of the 20th century set themselves was to improve the housing in which the people lived. This task is not yet complete: poverty still exists, both in the cities and the countryside, but the terrible tenements of the early 20th century have almost all disappeared. By the 1980s most Irish people had a standard of housing undreamed of by their grandparents. Even in the remotest parts of the country features such as electricity and indoor plumbing have come to be seen as normal.

In the post-war years, however, the effort to give all the people in cities an adequate standard of housing has run into trouble. The principal problem is the speed with which the urban population has grown, especially in the Dublin area. Most of the Republic's services are centralised in the capital, and by 1980 it had 30 per cent of the entire population

## FLAT SUBURBS, S.W., IN THE MORNING

The new red houses spring like plants
    In level rows
Of reddish herbage that bristles and slants
    Its square shadows.

The pink young houses show one side bright
    Flatly assuming the sun,
And one side shadow, half in sight,
    Half-hiding the pavement-run:

Where hastening creatures pass intent
    On their level way,
Threading like ants that can never relent
    And have nothing to say.

Bare stems of street lamps stiffly stand
    At random, desolate twigs,
To testify to a blight on the land
    That has stripped their sprigs.

*D. H. Lawrence*

*This cabin near Finglas Dublin provided adequate accommodation, by 19th century standards. In the 1980s, however, people have come to demand more substantial housing. Finglas is now one of the largest new housing areas, 100 years ago it was a remote rural area.*

and was still growing. Despite building nearly 18,000 houses and 6,500 flats between 1965 and 1980, Dublin Corporation still has not managed to provide enough housing for all.

## ASPECTS OF URBAN HOUSING

*Access:* The most immediate concern is access to housing. It is not easy to get onto a Corporation or Council housing list. Many people spend years waiting. At the same time, renting a privately-owned flat or trying to buy a house is too expensive for many. Loans and mortgages are available from banks and building societies which enable people to buy their own houses. To qualify for such loans it is necessary to be the holder of a 'steady' job.

*Ghettoes:* Modern urban housing tends to create ghettoes. Distinct areas of towns and cities can be separated on the basis of age and social class. In Dublin the Corporation has built vast estates to the north west, west and south west of the city to house working class families. Equally large estates have been built by private developers, especially on the south side. These are mainly occupied by young middle class families. Would it have been better to have built smaller and more mixed estates to give the city a more 'natural' balance?

| NUMBER ON DUBLIN CORPORATION'S HOUSING LIST, AWAITING PLACEMENT | |
|---|---|
| Before 1951 | No Housing List |
| 1951 | 10,000 (approx.) |
| 1956 | 6,520 |
| 1958 | 5,895 |
| 1960 | 6,823 |
| 1964 | 6,400 |
| 1968 | 5,301 |
| 1970 | 4,964 |
| 1972 | 5,307 |
| 1977 | 5,727 |
| 1980 | 5,463 |
| 1981 | 5,732 |
| 1982 | 6,228 (July 1982) |

*Source: Dublin Corporation*

**DUBLIN CORPORATION HOUSING SCHEMES**

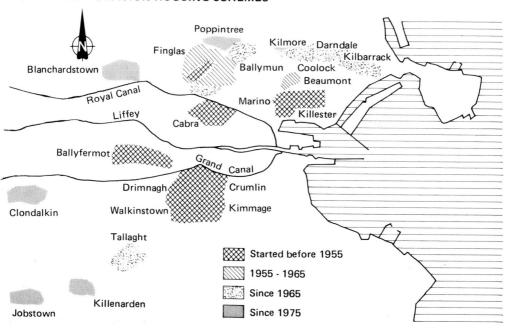

'Our street was a tough street, and the last outpost of toughness you'd meet as you left North Dublin for the red brick respectability of Jones's Road, Fitzroy Avenue, Clonliffe Road and Drumcondra generally.

Kids from those parts we despised, hated and resented. For the following sins: they lived in houses one to a family, which we thought greedy, unnatural and unsocial; they wore suits all the one colour, both jacket and pants, where we wore a jersey and shorts; they carried leather schoolbags where we either had a strap round our books or else a cheap check cloth bag.

Furthermore, it was suspected that some of them took piano lessons and dancing lessons, while we of the North Circular Road took anything we could lay our hands on which was not nailed down.

We brought one of them to our corner and bade him continue his performance, and thereafter any time we caught him, he was brought in bondage to the corner of Russell Street and invited to give a performance of the dance: hornpipe, jig, reel, or slip jig.

This young gent, in addition to being caught red-footed, was by colouring of hair red-headed, and I've often heard since that they are an exceedingly bad-tempered class of person which, signs on it, he was no exception. For having escaped from his exercises by reason of an approaching Civic Guard, by name 'Dirty Lug', he ran down to the canal bridge which was the border of our territory, and used language the like of which was shocking to anyone from Russell Street and guaranteed to turn thousands grey if they hailed from some other part.

However, our vengeance for the insults heaped upon us by this red-headed hornpiper, that thought so bad of giving the people an old step on the corner of the street, was not an empty one.

One day, not alone did we catch him, but he'd a jam roll under his oxter — steaming hot, crisp and sweet

He was a hidden villain all right. Long weeks after, myself and Scoil (or Skull, have it any way you fancy) Kane were moseying round Croker, not minding anything in particular. Kerry was playing Cavan in hurling or Derry was playing Tyrone in anything, but it wasn't a match of any great import to any save relations and friends, and a dilatory class of a Sunday afternoon was being had by all, when the Scoil (Skull) and myself were surrounded by a gang, if you please, from Jones's Road, and who but the red-headed dancing master at the head of them.

But we didn't take them seriously.

'Sound man, Jam Roll,' said I, not knowing what else to call him.

'I'll give you jam roll in a minute,' said Jam Roll.

'You're a dacent boy,' said I, 'and will you wet the tea as you're at it?'

'Will you stand out?' says Jam Roll.

'I will,' said I.

'In the cod or in the real?'

'The real,' said I; 'd' you take me for a hornpiper?'

He said no more but gave me a belt so that I thought the Hogan Stand had fallen on me. One off the ground. The real Bowery Belt.

'Now,' says he, when I came to, 'you won't call me Jam Roll again.'

'You were wrong there, Jam Roll.'

Brendan Behan: *Hold Your Hour*

from the bakery — and the shortest way from Summerhill to where he lived was through our street. He was tired, no doubt, with wearing suits and living in a house with only his own family and carrying that heavy leather schoolbag, not to mind the dancing lessons; no doubt he thought he had a right to be tired, and he took the shortest way home with the cake for his ma.

He could see none of our gang, but the fact that he didn't see us didn't mean we were not there. We were, as a matter of fact, playing 'the make in' on Brennan's Hill down by the Mountjoy Brewery when his approach was signalled by a scout, and in short order 'the make in' was postponed while we held up the red fellow and investigated his parcel.

We grabbed the booty, and were so intent on devouring the jam roll that we let the prisoner go over the bridge and home to plot his vengeance.

*Lifestyle:* Suburban houses are mass-produced and standardised, designed to suit the builder rather than the buyer. One is much the same as another, and modern districts take years to develop their own character. With the emphasis on building houses, facilities are often neglected. Nevertheless, suburbs offer everyone a comfortable and healthy environment, and are developing into vigorous new communities all over Ireland.

*Inner City Decline:* As a result of modern housing developments, inner city areas have lost their communities and much of their liveliness. As office blocks and expensive shopping areas have replaced homes and traditions, many parts of Ireland's large cities have become dark, deserted and dangerous. Ironically, inner-city housing is becoming fashionable among the well-to-do, especially since the energy crisis of the 1970s. Houses, originally built for labourers are now sold for prices that no labourer could even dream of, and 'select' new developments offer 'town houses' at extraordinary prices. Recently, however, Dublin Corporation has bowed to pressure from local communities, and has begun to re-house inner-city people in their own areas, and in houses that reflect the character of the various areas.

## WORK

After the expansion and euphoria of the 1960s came the recession and depression of the 1970s. The oil crisis of 1973/74, and the recession which followed, set the tone for the following decade. Expensive energy and inflation threw thousands out of work as companies went bankrupt, or economised to cut losses. Terms like 'short-time' and 'three-day week' came into everyday use. As less money was available, people bought less. As they did so, other industries were affected, and more jobs lost. This spiral continued, with only occasional breaks, into the 1980s.

The recession of the 1970s came on top of a deeper and more fundamental change that has been developing in modern industry since the war. Automation in various forms has been introduced into mass-production systems, and many jobs that were once carried out by people are now done by machines. The invention of the microchip has speeded up this process. The microchip has enabled engineers to build very accurate and compact machines that are cheaper and more efficient to employ than people.

## BIDDY MULLIGAN

I'm a buxom fine widow I live in a spot
In Dublin they call it the Coombe
Me shop and me stall are laid out on the street
And me palace consists of one room
I sell apples and oranges, nuts and split peas
Bananas and sugar stick sweets
On Saturday night I sell second hand clothes
From the flure of one stall on the street.

CHORUS:
You may travel from Clare to the Co. Kildare
From Francis Street on to Macroom,
But where would you see a fine widow like me
Biddy Mulligan the pride of the Coombe.

I sell fish on a Friday set out on a board
The finest you'd find in the sea
But the best is me herrins, fine
    Dublin Bay herrins
It's herrins for dinner today
I have a son Mick and he's great on the flute
He plays in the Longford Street Band
It would do your heart good to see him
    march out
On a Sunday for Dollymount Strand.

CHORUS:

In the Park on a Sunday I make quite a dash
The neighbours look on with surprise
With me Aberdeen shawlie thrown over
    me head
I dazzle the sight of their eyes.
At Patrick Street corner for 64 years
I stood and no one can deny
That while I stood there no person
    dare say
That black was the white of me eye.

CHORUS:

An old-style industrial country like Britain is particularly badly hit by this development, because its factories were built when fuel and labour were cheap. They have huge assembly lines, and outmoded production systems. New technology is reducing the need for large numbers of people on the assembly lines, and causing wide-spread redundancies with very serious effects on the whole economy. A newly-industrialised country like Ireland is not so badly affected. However, the new technology affects plans for future industries. New factories no longer mean employment for the large number of people they used to, as the fully mechanised processes and robot assembly-lines, now possible, cost less than human labour.

*Electronics are having a profound influence in the 1980s.*

### THE CHANGING DISTRIBUTION OF THE WORKFORCE IN THE REPUBLIC OF IRELAND

**Table 1**  Distribution of Workforce

|  | 1926 % | 1946 % | 1964 % | 1980 % | 2000* % |
|---|---|---|---|---|---|
| Agriculture | 54 | 46 | 33 | 19 | 12 |
| Industry | 13 | 19 | 27 | 32 | 37 |
| Services | 33 | 35 | 40 | 49 | 51 |

*projected

**Table 2**  Industry by Sectors (1980)

| Sector | Rep. of Ireland % | EEC % |
|---|---|---|
| Food, Drink & Tobacco | 26 | 9 |
| Textiles, Clothing & Footwear | 17 | 15 |
| Wood & Furniture | 3 | 5 |
| Paper & Printing | 5 | 6 |
| Chemicals | 6 | 10 |
| Clay Products | 7 | 5 |
| Metals & Engineering | 29 | 48 |
| Other | 7 | 2 |
| Total | 100 | 100 |

*Source: Confederation of Irish Industry*

The same change is beginning to appear in white-collar and service employment. This has very serious implications for the Republic of Ireland, where there is a very large proportion of service jobs. The impact can already be seen in the changes in the recruitment programmes of large firms, the banks and the Civil Service These have always been major employers, and each year took several thousand school-leavers on to their staffs. However, computer technology is replacing many of the jobs these school-leavers would have done.

● With a simple computerised system a firm can keep records of its stocks, outlay, expenses, invoices and receipts. *At risk:* store-clerks, invoice clerks, and book-keepers.

● Word processors, simply computer-ised typewriters, can store and automatically type circular letters. They can also make corrections or alterations at the push of a button. *At risk:* thousands of typists.

- Since 1980 it has been possible for an Irish firm to use a telephone that can be programmed to dial numbers repeatedly until it is answered. *At risk:* receptionists and secretaries.

- In television stations, programme-makers can use computerised control desks that will, at the push of a button, perform jobs that previously took several workers days to complete. *At risk:* film editors, production assistants.

Supermarkets will soon introduce a completely computerised stocklisting system that will keep a complete and accurate record of their stocks, down to advising when orders should be renewed. Such a system would mean that there would be no jobs for store-clerks or stock-takers. If the computer were able to place the new orders, as most will be, then more jobs will be affected. In some systems, even the store room will be staffed by robots, and invoices and payments will be made by the computer.

**STOCKS.** The Computer can record all incoming and outgoing stock. If stocks on record fall below a certain level, the computer orders more from suppliers, often simply by notifying the latter's own computers.

**CONSUMER**

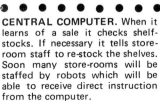

**CENTRAL COMPUTER.** When it learns of a sale it checks shelf-stocks. If necessary it tells store-room staff to re-stock the shelves. Soon many store-rooms will be staffed by robots which will be able to receive direct instruction from the computer.

000127 161092

All products will have a computer coding like this which is designed so that it can be read by a computer.

**WAGES, BILLS.** The computer makes out wages and cheques. It also checks and pays bills from suppliers.

**CHECKOUT.** This is linked to the computer. It scans the code on each product and notifies the sale to the computer.

The advance of new technology arouses mixed reactions. Some people argue that the jobs that are being done by robots and computers are mostly boring, repetitive jobs. They maintain that the technology offers a world without drudgery, and that it will free the creative talents of the human race. Others argue that the new technology is creating a world built around machines rather than people. They see the machines putting people out of jobs, simply because of their reliability and economy. This, they argue, is putting profits before people, and shows a lack of social responsibility.

The question is a complex one. Computer technology is going to shape the future, and any industry that ignores it will not last long. At the same time, people in Europe and North America place great importance on their jobs. Sometimes it even seems that they only exist in terms of the jobs they perform. We are all expected to *be* something, like a cook, a mechanic, a clerk, a housewife, an architect, a television star. Anybody who is unemployed automatically loses this kind of identity, and very often their self-respect goes with it. As a result, any technology that does away with large numbers of jobs, however boring or menial they may be, must be carefully controlled.

MEETING THE CHALLENGE

In the end it falls to the government to oversee the change and to ensure that it happens fast enough to protect industry, but not so quickly that people are threatened.

*Training in required skills:* While un-

NATIONAL MANPOWER SERVICE

VACANCY DATA: JANUARY 1 – MARCH 31, 1981

| *Occupational Group* | *Number of posts unfilled at end of March, 1981* |
|---|---|
| Managerial and support occupations | 113 |
| Education, arts, health and sports occupations | 67 |
| Engineering and technology professionals | 126 |
| Production and Service manager | 70 |
| Clerical and related occupations | 305 |
| Selling occupations | 183 |
| Personal service occupations | 391 |
| Farming, fishing and related occupations | 23 |
| Processing, making and repairing occupations, (excluding metal and electrical) | 278 |
| Processing, making and repairing occupations (metal and electrical) | 220 |
| Construction and general factory operatives | 301 |
| Transport and storage occupations | 98 |
| Miscellaneous occupations | 157 |
| Apprenticeship vacancies | 29 |
| Total | 2,361* |

*NB. This is not the national total of unfilled jobs. It is the number of vacancies notified to the National Manpower Service.

employment is a very serious problem in Ireland, and further jobs will be lost through new technology, there are still jobs left unfilled because there are serious shortages of skilled manpower in certain areas.

Large numbers of unfilled jobs mean that firms cannot work at their full potential, and earnings are lost. If these jobs were filled, their spin-off would create more jobs. In other words, the people who filled the jobs would have salaries to spend. This would increase the demand for various goods and services, which would lead to the creation of yet more jobs.

It is important that young people are made aware of the areas where vacancies are occurring to that they can consider what sort of education they need. Training opportunities must be created so that people with general skills can be trained or re-trained for specific jobs.

*Development of Small Industries:* Since the industrial expansion of the 1960s, the Industrial Development Authority has concentrated on jobs in large-scale industries, as it is felt that the more jobs a single negotiating process can give, the better. Politicians also like the large figures involved. Headlines reading '2000 NEW JOBS FOR BANTRY' are good publicity for whoever is in government.

Unfortunately, the grants that the IDA has to pay for foreign firms to attract them to Ireland can make job creation very expensive. As a result there is renewed interest in smaller industries.

Small firms have a very clear understanding of their market. While their profit margins are often tighter than large companies, they have much greater flexibility. Furthermore, many are in the craft area, or cater for minority or luxury markets which tend to be dependable.

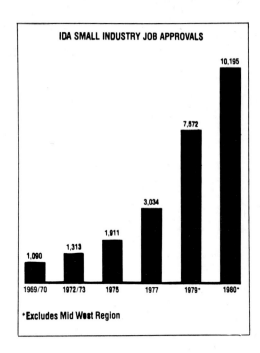

**IDA SMALL INDUSTRY JOB APPROVALS**

| | |
|---|---|
| 1969/70 | 1,090 |
| 1972/73 | 1,313 |
| 1975 | 1,911 |
| 1977 | 3,034 |
| 1979* | 7,572 |
| 1980* | 10,195 |

*Excludes Mid West Region

*Development of New Industries:* Some of Ireland's most important traditional industries, such as clothing and footwear, have great difficulties in fighting foreign competition. There is even a call for a return to the policy of protecting Irish-made goods by taxing imports, although this is against EEC regulations. A strong 'buy Irish' campaign has been launched in the media to make people aware that, by buying Irish-made goods, they are helping to protect jobs.

Since older industries find it difficult to survive, it is necessary to find others which are more suited to the 1980s and 1990s. Among the most fruitful industries for the future are computer technology, pharmaceutical and health-care products, electronics and leisure products.

*Changes in Work Practices:* If the amount of work available in the future is limited, it may prove necessary to change some of the ways we organise ourselves for work:

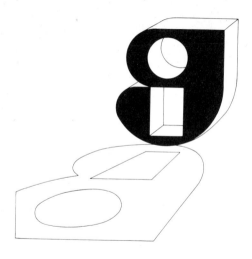

- *Less overtime* — If there is wide-spread unemployment, is it justifiable for workers to do extra work for extra pay? Would it be fairer to share the work out among more workers? It still suits many firms to have overtime; they find it cheaper and easier to organise.

- *A shorter working week* — The length of the working week has fallen steadily since the 19th century. If it continued to fall, it would free more work hours for other workers. However, employers tend to resist this idea, as they feel it would lower the productivity of each worker.

- *Longer holidays* — EEC regulations have steadily lengthened the worker's annual leave. The effect of longer holidays is to free work for other workers.

- *Early retirement* — This would take workers out of the competition for jobs, and leave more scope for younger workers. A major problem with early retirement is the fact that people, especially those near retirement age, tend to see themselves in terms of their

---

**BAILEYS:**

*— An Irish Success Story*

While there are difficulties for some Irish industries, others have developed new products that have proved spectacularly successful. Many of these derive their strength from particular Irish qualities. The most extraordinary triumph in Irish industry in the 1970s was based on two of Ireland's most traditional industries, distilling and dairy farming.

The Irish drinks company, Gilbeys, launched a new product on the market in 1974. A sweet mixture of Irish whiskey, Irish cream and subtle flavours, it was called Bailey's Irish Cream. Their initial target was to sell 25,000 cases a year, expanding to 50 – 100,000 by 1980. Instead, by 1978 they were selling 500,000 cases a year.

In 1979 the product was launched in the United States. In 1981 250,000 cases were sold there and in 1981 600,000. Annual output has risen to 2,000,000 cases by 1981; 95 per cent of these, worth almost £60,000,000, are exported, that is 67 per cent of all Irish alcohol exports, and 1 per cent of all Irish exports.

A product like Baileys Irish Cream has vast significance for many areas. Hundreds of jobs have been created in Dublin. Farmers have reason to be pleased as well, as Baileys uses the cream of 26,000,000 gallons of milk a year, which is a major boost for the dairy industry.

However, perhaps the product's main significance, lies in the unique combination of originality and tradition.

jobs. Their job is their identity. Many workers do not live long past retirement. If workers are to retire earlier, it will be necessary to prepare them for life after work.

*Attitudes to work:* All of these suggestions may ease the problems of employment, but many workers may soon have to face an even more radical question: *What is a job, and is everyone entitled to one?* Irish people, like other Europeans, see a person's job as his or her most important activity. If large numbers of people are underemployed, we will have to change this attitude.

*Leisure:* is the time we have to ourselves. Since the industrial revolution took work away from the home, people have thought of leisure time as time spent doing things they want to do out of work. Sometimes this is more work, sometimes it is another occupation entirely, sometimes it is nothing at all.

Changes in work practices — shorter working week, longer holidays, earlier retirement — will dramatically affect our ideas of leisure time. An increasingly larger part of our lives will be spent out of work.

Does Irish society prepare people for using their leisure time? The pub can seem the centre of our social activities (in 1980 £700 million was spent on alcohol in the Republic of Ireland). In rural areas, social life is often trapped in the triangle of pub, dance-hall and sportsfield.

Urban areas are better off for leisure facilities, but it is usually left to private or local enterprise to provide them. Discos, concerts, cinemas, pubs, race meetings and bingo sessions are organised for profit by business people; night classes are provided for a small fee by local education organisations.

Some Irish suburbs have strong community or tenant organisations who co-ordinate the building of community centres with swimming pools, gymnasiums and games rooms. Many of these centres have areas where plays can be rehearsed or performed, music played and classes given. However, many areas have no community centre, or community sense. Is it fair that the provision of facilities and organisations should be left to depend on the energy and dedication of unpaid volunteers?

Government agencies have been slow to involve themselves in planning for leisure. The Department of Education has a section with responsibility for sport, but this tends to concentrate on outdoor activities. This is highly important, especially in urban areas where many people have indoor jobs, but it is still only one aspect of leisure.

Do we place too much importance on the time spent in our workplace and not enough on the time spent away from it? When we remember the increasing amount of leisure time available to workers, and the opportunities these offer for new leisure industries, should there be some kind of development authority for leisure activities and industries?

111

## E L E A N O R   R I G B Y

Ah, look at all the lonely people,
Ah, look at all the lonely people.
Eleanor Rigby picks up the rice in the
   church where a wedding has been,
lives in a dream.
Waits at the window, wearing a face
   that she keeps
in a jar by the door,
Who is it for?
All the lonely people, where do they
   all come from?
All the lonely people, where do they
   all belong?
Father McKenzie, writing the words of
   a sermon that no-one will hear,
No-one comes near
Look at him working, darning his
   socks in the night
when there's nobody there,

What does he care?
All the lonely people, where do they
   all come from?
All the lonely people, where do they
   all belong?
Ah, look at all the lonely people.
Ah, look at all the lonely people.
Eleanor Rigby died in the church and
   was buried along with her name.
Nobody came.
Father McKenzie, wiping the dirt from
   his hands as he walks from the grave.
No-one was saved.
All the lonely people, where do they
   all come from?
All the lonely people, where do they
   all belong?

*John Lennon and
Paul McCartney*

## GROWING UP IN DUBLIN
Noel McFarlane wrote this portrait
of a city boy when he was 17.

'Dublin, and the beerbarrels pushed from the laden trucks chimed with the churches. And the cornerboys, who propped the walls of the bookies' secret dens, and watched the smug and smokey city, seldom moved. We walked past them in the quiet of reverence, as though it were a shrine we passed, or a ghostly spot. These were the gloomy men that fathers slyly pointed to and told us we'd end up like in the finish if we mitched — low cornerboys, chasing woodbine butts in the gutter, and keeping the unfortunate taxpayers of the nation doubled-up crooked getting fleeced with taxes. O them's the boys to give a wide berth to, they said, backing horses all the long day, and keeping the publicans fat.

But to us they were lofty Gods, and we loafed at our own corner, imitating their few gestures, squeezing strings of forbidden curses through the

*Many thousands are employed at the Port of Dublin.*

corners of our mouths and teeth we imagined black, thinking ourselves the ruination of teachers and the unfortunate taxpayers, smoking brazen butts and spitting. Mush, our gang-leader, harboured no other ambition than to grow up and decorate the bookie's wall in Ballyfermot. He was maybe ten, and a year older than the rest of us, but spoke and acted three times his age. He wanted to be a bowsie, a professional bowsie, and explained: 'Look, it's dead easy. You just get set up with a mot, produce the couple of chisellers, and you're on the pig's back. A gentleman of leisure, no less.'

We watched him in awe that was vainly hidden, and marvelled as he stole the egg from the same doddering shopkeeper at the same time every Saturday afternoon, to throw in the darkness of the picturehouse, and he would be impassive and innocent in the flickering light of the screen as the shocked victim was ushered past our seat, festooned in rich syrup, as the elephants hailed out Tarzan. Once, as the lights lowered on a tale of buck-toothed Dracula, he produced two frightened racing pigeons from his pocket and cast them over the rows of children's heads screaming as they flapped in the murk 'It's the vampires, Jaysus, it's the vampires.' When the havoc quietened, and the children calmed, he produced a pipe, and commenced to puff.

In winter, when we scraped the rare frost off the walls for the warm napes of girls, we would call for Mush on the white way to school. His head, muffled in blankets, would appear at the bedroom window.

Was he going? We were not to be making disturbances, he said, at this hour of the night, and the Da only after going to bed and was up all the night on the gargle. And to tell that big ignorant baluba of a mulchie in the school that the grandfather was after getting a right feed of Dunlop crossing the road, and was dead, and Mush was obliged to pay his respects and he mightn't be in tomorrow either. Or if we didn't like that one, think up something on the way. And the head would sleepily withdraw, replaced by a shivering hand closing the window against the chill, and the unpleasing thoughts of school. When he did condescend to appear, covered in horsehair from the gypsie's nags, he would drum loudly with his filthy nails on his initiated desklid, or snuggle closely to the warm pipes and snooze.

And then one Monday morning Mush sheepishly entered the class and said that he had reformed. His washed and shining face was viewed with shock as he explained that his dead uncle had appeared to him in a dream. His uncle, himself a former professional bowsie, had told him that the dicey life he was leading was not for the likes of him, and a little bit of hard graft would do him a power of good. In a day Mush was putting up his hand. In two days he was answering. And on the third day Mush was collecting for The Black Babies. That Saturday, in the darkness of the picturehouse, Mush chainsmoked fat cigars. When the principal, a pious man, who said the prayers with his eyes shut, slammed into the class, having opened the collection box to count the monthly offering, and emptied the contents onto the teacher's desk, there issued therefrom, in a dancing bronze torrent, a good selection of plumbers washers, it was noticed that Mush had made an exit, as meekly as he entered.

Mush could be seen now more and more, clattering up Ballyfermot Road on a huge and haggard and gasping mare, borrowed from the coalman, to place his own and his father's bets, who was also a prominent professional bowsie, and he usually didn't bother to dismount at the door, but would urge his sweating steed inside with a nudge of his knees and wait in the line of stunned men, then, frowning at the yellowed clock, he would clatter home, for the two-o'clock.

Mothers clucked warnings: 'Have no truck with that maneen', fathers gave promises of warnings if we did, mistrusting his tattered clothes, the sleeve of his jumper stiff with mucus, and the vermin he hunted in his matted hair. But still we hungered for his rare and benign nod of approval, and he, in turn, basked in our homage. Then, on an autumn day, Mush, the wild leader, the foxy tactitian, collapsed into a child, like the rest of us. The trees spread like webs over us as we gathered our harvest of empty cider bottles for the refund. Mush supervised and urged us with chatter, sensing our nervousness under the drooping trees, in the stillness, broken only by the timid tinkle of the bottles.

Then we saw Mush staring at the ground, bending slowly and speaking soft curses, and with shyness patting a tuft of grass. It trembled under us, a young deer, still wet from it's mother, falling from it's crooked legs, and fearing us. We looked to Mush and Mush looked at the deer, with indecision, faltering, with fear. When finally he stretched a hand to fondle the doe crashed back on it's side and strove urgently for breath. He stood back into our tiny circle, into our silent vigil, and he watched the doe gasp and clamour for breath. We followed him when he burst out of the forest, crashing through the dry bron of leaves and tumbling down the steepness of the hill and through the mucky acres of grass to the gate-

man's house. Mush hammered with fury, and he came, wrapped in grumbles and old, clutching with mistrust his stern and straight stick. We crowded, worried him with voices.

There was a little deer up in the forest and . . .

What were we doing up in forest? Were we up to something?

No, no, no, there was a little deer and it couldn't stand . . .

Were we from Ballyfermot? Breaking his trees?

It can't breathe even . . .

Lighting fires and rampaging, little bowsies. He'd get the guards.

But the deer . . .

He worried us to the gate with his stick. Mush spitting and dodging and jeering into his deaf ears.

There were many such deaf-heads discovered as the seasons turned, and Mush, his rotten fangs showing, his eyes crazed with cheap wine, would probe and attack through instinct.

Mush was very proud of his teeth, incidentally, and would grin his black and yellow grin into shopwindows and mirrors, admiring his proper bowsies leer, and telling the stories of his scars and absent teeth.

In the last year of primary school, when the School Inspector, a tall man with a spy's seedy raincoat, called to his house. Mush chased him for two miles with an antique sword, prodding his plump buttocks, and shouting he was Brian Boru, after giving a lep up out of the grave. Charge: Assault, the Probation Act. Not two months later, while visiting relatives in the vicinity of Sean McDermott St. Mush strained the cabbage on the 'polis', from an upper storey balcony, severely scalding a guard, case dismissed.

Mush began to spend his days in town, while we attended tech., and said that there was a great shower of hooks knocking around, and the little chisellers hardly able to walk could strip a lorry like ants while it was stopped at the traffic lights, and the polis took their life into their hands going into where the grannie lived, and when you went in there they never went in after you. It was like crossing the border into Mexico.

We saw little of him then, and were guilty in our thankfulness, but we read his name in the papers, and the charges, and he said that when he went into St. Pats it was for 'Refresher Courses'. I met Mush recently in town, outside a chip shop, a professional bowsie, tapping up, and he told me that there was 'A shower of gobshites out of the college, with big beards and Sandymount lawdy-daw, saying that they were here to help me. Lord, you can't piss crooked without them, where the grannie lives, tripping over them, no less.' He said he'd got a whole dose of books out of one fellow's car the other day, and they were going cheap. Was I interested?'

*Noel McFarlane*

*Earlsfort Terrace, Dublin, 1982. Some people feel that vandalism and a lack of social responsibility is not confined to graffiti-writers. The 'developers' of this site knocked down its fine old buildings, left the site for over a decade without building anything. Yet, the site's value increased by many millions of pounds.*

Modern urban life is in many ways a magical and glamorous existence. However, the surface can mask a great deal of misery and difficulty. Violence is common, both on the streets and in the home. Robbery is an everyday offence, and no street escapes the attention of vandals for long, particularly in the most depressed urban area, the inner city.

Huge areas are being redeveloped. Old streets, once used for housing and neighbourhood shops, are being pulled down to make way for multistorey office blocks and luxury shopping centres, few of which have any human existence after 6.00 p.m.

Modern town-planning locates new housing and industrial estates in growing suburbs and 'new towns', and inner-city areas are starved of jobs. Unemployment rates are therefore very high, and prospects for employment poor.

Taken all-in-all, many centre-city developments, such as shopping centres and wider streets, are improving the overall standard of city life. However, from the point of view of the inner-city dweller, their effects are often negative.

Problems are not confined to inner-city areas. Public leisure facilities are often the last thing to be installed in a new estate. Sometimes the first row of houses will have stood for six or seven years before a playground or green area is prepared. The authorities usually argue that this is because they do not officially take over responsibility for an area until building is completed. They also suffer from shortages of money. However, this is small consolation for children who have nowhere to play, and their parents.

New suburbs also suffer from a lack of night-time leisure facilities. Since the 1970s and 1980s, for instance, most cinemas have been centralised in the city and residents of large suburbs have to travel 15 or 20 kilometres to visit them. There are few venues where people can listen to live music, except for pubs. Although discos are far more widespread, they also tend to be concentrated in town centres.

Certain groups of people are especially vulnerable:

- Young people feel trapped in large sprawling areas that have no facilities for them. With nowhere to play, they hang around on street corners where they fall foul of police and shopkeepers. Many see no prospects of employment, and regard their education as a waste of time. Living in overcrowded homes and characterless areas, they sometimes express their anger and frustration in violence and vandalism.

- Ghetto areas develop the reputation of being 'tough' and people living there become demoralised.

- Many housewives live their lives in kitchens and bedrooms in faceless suburban estates. Trapped by their circumstances and without creche facilities, they often have no way of developing their own talents.

- Another group of angry people in any large town are the commuters, who spend hours each day stuck in traffic jams on their way to and from work.

- The most defenceless urban group is the poor. In a society that places so much value on consumerism and spending, that values wealth and success above all else, it is hardly surprising that the poor

and the unemployed feel angry and frustrated. In a society that respects the haves, they are the have nots.

- Obviously, there are other, more private, causes for a person turning to crime. However, deprivation undoubtedly plays a major part.

CRIME RATES 1980

| Area | Number of crimes per 1,000 people |
|---|---|
| Carlow/Kildare | 9.9 |
| Cavan/Monaghan | 6.7 |
| Cork East | 24.3 |
| Cork West | 5.4 |
| Clare | 8.7 |
| Donegal | 8.2 |
| Galway West | 12.2 |
| Kerry | 10.3 |
| Leix/Offaly | 9.9 |
| Limerick | 18.9 |
| Longford6E | |
| Longford/Westmeath | 15.7 |
| Louth/Meath | 19.7 |
| Mayo | 5.3 |
| Roscommon/Galway East | 4.9 |
| Sligo/Leitrim | 9.0 |
| Tipperary | 13.9 |
| Waterford/Kilkenny | 9.9 |
| Wexford | 17.5 |
| Dublin Metropolitan Areas — | |
| Northern | 16.8 |
| North Central | 163.9 |
| South Central | 114.2 |
| Southern | 26.6 |
| Eastern | 25.4 |

*Source: Report on Crime 1980*
Garda Siochana

## CRIME IN DUBLIN CITY

The Dublin Metropolitan Area has:

- 29.8% of the total population of the Republic of Ireland
- 57.4% of all indictable offences recorded.
- 37.0% of all offences against the person (e.g. murder, manslaughter, dangerous driving causing death, assault).
- 54.4% of all offences against property with violence (e.g. robbery, burglary, arson, malicious damage).
- 60.1% of all larcenies (stealing)
- 88.3% of all other offences.

*Source: Report on Crime 1980*
*Garda Síochána*

Many people are now beginning to ask whether the media have played a role in increasing crime, especially violent crime. Newspapers and television tend to concentrate on the more grisly stories they have reports on. TV fictional series often present violence and robbery as socially acceptable. Many observers think that media coverage of events in Northern Ireland has affected attitudes in the Republic, and that petrol bombs, riots and murders do not seem as shocking as they did ten years ago, because people have become used to them.

At the same time, many people who have less obvious reasons to be discontented are also unhappy. The fast lifestyle can seem empty and pointless. During the 1960s and 1970s many people opted out of what they called the rat-race, and moved into other kinds of work. Civil servants became potters, teachers became craftshop owners, engineers became goat farmers.

Many suggestions have been made as to how the problem of disaffec-

tion in our cities can be tackled. How realistic are they?

*More law and order:* Do we need more police and harsher laws to make our homes and streets safe?

*Better employment prospects:* Many people gain in self-esteem when working. But would more employment mean less crime?

*More facilities for the young:* A lot of random vandalism is carried out by youngsters with nothing to do. But do they want to have something to do? If there were better facilities in local areas, would that reduce the level of vandalism?

*Education:* Could our schools do more to prepare pupils for life in the modern world? Do they give a sense of being a member of a community, or of being part of a city's life? Do pupils learn enough about drug use? What do school-goers learn about vandalism?

*Changing society:* Is the answer in the long run to change society, making it less impersonal and consumerist and more caring and communal. But how is this to be achieved?

## The Unknown Citizen

*(To JS/07/M378 This Marble Monument*
*is Erected by the State)*

He was found by the Bureau of Statistics
    to be
One against whom there was no official
    complaint,
And all the reports of his conduct agree
That, in the modern sense of an old-
    fashioned word, he was a saint,
For in everything he did he served the
    Greater Community.
Except for the War till the day he retired
He worked in a factory and never got fired,
But satisfied his employers, Fudge Motors Inc.
Yet he wasn't a scab or odd in his views,
For his Union reports that he paid his dues,
(Our report on his Union shows it was sound)
And our Social Psychology workers found
That he was popular with his mates and
    liked a drink.
The Press are convinced that he bought a
    paper every day
And that his reactions to advertisements
    were normal in every way.
Policies taken out in his name prove that
    he was fully insured,
And his Health-card shows that he was
    once in hospital but left it cured.

Both Producers Research and High-Grade
    Living declare
He was fully sensible to the advantages of
    the Instalment Plan
And had everything necessary to the Modern
    Man,
A phonograph, a radio, a car and a frigidaire.
Our researchers into Public Opinion are
    content
That he held the proper opinions for the
    time of year;
When there was peace, he was for peace;
    when there was war, he went.
He was married and added five children to
    the population,
Which our Eugenist says was the right
    number for a parent of his generation,
And our teachers report that he never inter-
    fered with their education.
Was he free? Was he happy? The question
    is absurd:
Had anything been wrong, we should
    certainly have heard.

*W. H. Auden*

## LIVING WITH CHANGE

As we have seen, Ireland is in the middle of one of the most important changes in its history. All around are the sights and sounds of a new urban Ireland. Much of the environment and the lifestyle our grandparents knew have disappeared. All is changed utterly.

Once-familiar city streets disappear with monotonous regularity to be re-furbished with new glasshouse office blocks. Old shops close, new ones open, many with cross-channel links. Brand names change, streetnames change, landscapes change, fields dis-appear under streams of concrete. Communities are uprooted and trans-ported to what is, for them, the country.

Each day brings an avalanche of technological developments, many of them replacing other recent arrivals. In 1970 it would have taken a room-sized computer to carry out functions that can now be performed by one the size of a typewriter. In 1975 most television sets had six channels; in 1980 the most advanced offer twenty.

Buildings and cars which were designed in the 1960s assumed a never-ending supply of oil; later, people became much more energy-conscious and this has influenced most plans since then, bringing about yet more changes.

Change, too, can be found in ideas and attitudes. As we have seen, things which people had accepted for centur-ies about how they should live, and society organised, were strongly challenged. Later, in the 1970s, more conservative viewpoints returned as the economic recession began to be felt.

People's feelings about this constant change depends on their background, their education, and most of all, their attitude towards life itself. There are those who welcome turmoil and find the opportunities opened up by change as exciting. Others, content in their ways, find change disturbing and unpleasant. There is, however, very little anyone can do to prevent it. Not only has the individual lost control of change, but the speed with which it is occurring is getting faster all the time, faster than any educational or re-training schemes can match.

*Part Five*
# CITIES IN THE FUTURE

### Ireland in the Year 2000?

The population of the Irish Republic will have risen to 4.1 million. The Greater Dublin area will have 1,250,000 people. The east coast will have over 40 per cent of the national population.

In 1980 one person in every five had a car. In 2000 one in every three will have one, if present trends continue.

A modest 3-bedroom semi-detached house will cost £100,000.

By law, houses built in Switzerland must have a fallout shelter. In Ireland, no effort has yet been made to develop ways of protecting the population from a nuclear attack. Will this still continue to be the case in 2000?

IT'S A PITY THE OIL RAN OUT...BUT STILL IT GIVES ME GREAT PLEASURE TO FINALLY DECLARE...

DUBLIN 1999

While planners plan and scientists test, life must go on. Visions of 'ideal' urban environments demand immense co-ordination and large-scale planning. It is easy to design a new area, or a small urban complex like Dublin's Irish Life complex in Talbot Street. But to do so on a larger scale could take generations, as sites have to be bought up bit by bit, transport re-routed, communities re-housed, and so on. In general, it becomes too ambitious and too costly to think of vast new cities, and the chances are that instead of jumping into Utopia, city life will stumble on much as it has in the past.

Urban life will be different in the 21st century: of that there is no doubt. However, changes will probably be haphazard and unco-ordinated. Startling breakthroughs in technology may quickly and efficiently solve our present urban problems; they may, on the other hand, just create new problems. Planning for the future of our cities can only be based on what people know from the present. With constant change all around, any realistic planning becomes very difficult indeed.

### AFTER THE TIME OF PLENTY

'Mostly, of course, we wanted to know what was happening in the territories to the east and to the south — referred to as 'out there' or 'down there' — because we knew that what happened there would sooner or later affect us. We had to know what gangs were approaching, or rumoured to be approaching — gangs which, as I've said, were not all 'kids' and 'youngsters' now, were made up of every kind and age of person, were more and more tribes, were the new social unit; we had to know what

Cartoon by Richard Willson, 'The Ecologist'. By the year 2000, 18 cities in developing countries will each have a population of over 10 million. Over half the people on earth will be living in urban areas. Mexico City will have 31 million, Sao Paolo and Tokyo-Yokohama will have 26 million each. The great urban areas of Britain and the United States have also had major problems.

shortages were expected or might be abating; if another suburb had decided entirely to turn its back on gas, electricity and oil and revert to candle power and ingenuity; if a new rubbish dump had been found, and if so, could ordinary people get access to its riches; where there were shops that might have hides or old blankets or rose hips for vitamin syrups, or recycled plastic objects, or metal things like sieves and saucepans, or whatever it was, whatever might be cast up from the dead time of plenty.

Of course, such contriving and patching and making do began to parallel our ordinary living, our affluence and waste and overeating, at a very early stage, long before the time of which I am writing now. We were all experts at making a great

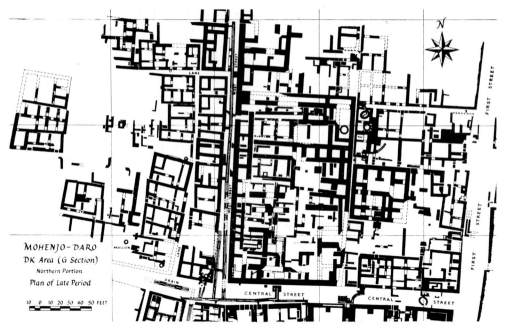

*Mohenjo-daro on the Indus River, 3000 B.C.*

deal out of very little, even while we all still had a lot, and were still being incited by advertisements to spend and use and discard.

Sometimes I left Emily — fearful, of course, for what might happen in my absence, but thinking the risk worth it — to make trips a good way out from the city, to villages, farms, other towns. These might take two or three days, since the trains and buses were so infrequent and unreliable, and the cars, nearly all of them used by officialdom, so reluctant to offer lifts because of the fear of ordinary people felt by the official class. I walked, having rediscovered the uses of my feet, like most people.'

Doris Lessing: *Memoirs of a Survivor*

## FUTURE CITIES

For most people, the future is an extension of the present. It may be brighter, faster, more polluted, or changed in some other way, but is seen by most as similar to the life-style we live now.

This may not be the case. Mankind's growing population, continued search for resources and increasing technological expertise may all lead to the need or demand for a very different type of urban development in the future.

## THE URBAN VILLAGE

One example of the alternative approach is in the idea of a city as a combination of a number of small communities, or villages, each having its own urban system of housing areas, leisure amenities, shopping centres, workplaces and so on. The emphasis here is on *smallness*.

## THE GARDEN CITY

Many city-dwellers are attracted to the idea of a garden city, with electric public transport moving people quietly through a landscape that places the emphasis on trees, shrubs and flowers, and generally on providing a peaceful atmosphere for people to live in. This idea was first

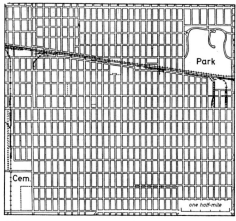

*Chicago, USA, late 20th century A.D.*

proposed by Ebenezer Howard. A number of suburban centres in Britain have been built on its principles.

### GOING UNDERGROUND

In the near future we are likely to see a new style of public building, which will be largely constructed underground, where it is a simple matter to maintain light and heat. Such buildings would have low-rise sections overground, probably heated by solar panels. When applied on a large scale, this could mean huge sections of major cities being built underground.

### DOMED CITIES

Another option for the future is the development of cities or units of cities shielded by large transparent plastic domes supported by warm air. These would allow controlled atmosphere in the areas they cover. Pollution would be excluded, and an even temperature maintained. It is already planned that domes like this, but on a smaller scale, will be erected over some of the world's larger sports stadiums in the late 1980s, and they will mean that playing surfaces can be maintained free from excessive flooding or drought.

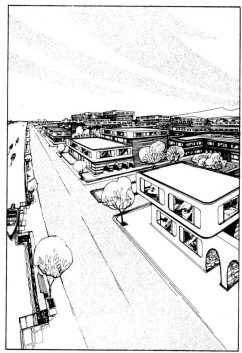

*From 'Studies in Long Term Development of the Port of Dublin'.*

### CITIES IN ORBIT

A generation has elapsed since mankind's first giant step into space, and some of its possibilities are now beginning to be understood. Not all of these are pleasant. The USA and the USSR have spent as much money on developing spy satellites and space weaponry as they have on exploration and scientific analysis.

Fortunately, the move to space will not only be for military purposes. Scientists have suggested ways in

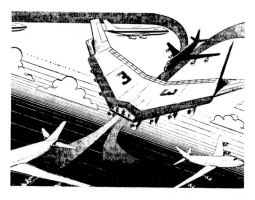

*A mining complex on Io, volcanic moon of Jupiter in the film 'Outland'.*

which the sun's energy could be gathered by giant solar panels in space and beamed back to earth. Such giant space power-stations would also include factory complexes where disposal of pollution and waste would be no problem.

Men have already spent considerable amounts of time in space, living in small space-stations. Within the next century, as the size of these orbiting stations increases greatly, they will begin to adopt some of the style of cities, with living areas, sport and entertainment complexes, even shopping centres.

### UNDER THE SEA?

The sea remains largely unexplored by man. Yet it seems certain that it harbours a vast store of resources, from coal and oil to possibilities of marine farming. Within the next century people may well live and work in underwater cities enclosed in giant bubbles and heated and warmed by underwater power stations that also feed overground cities.

*(Dublin Opinion)*

**LABOUR AND SPACE-SAVING DEVICE (PATENT REFUSED).**

Combined Gas Cooker, Dog-kennel, Gramophone, Meat Safe, Clock, Hat-Stand, and Child's Money-Box for use in those small modern houses.

### BACK TO NATURE?

Already many people have decided to reject the pace and problems of urban living. They have started new lives in remote rural areas, producing what they need from the land and by their own labour. If their lifestyle remains very simple, they can be independent of many of the outside forces which control other people's lives — employment, money, availability and cost of consumer goods, changes on the world market, especially in oil, etc. With resources becoming scarcer and the problems of city life more pressing, it could well be that more and more people will choose a life of self-sufficiency.

*'Corbusier is all very fine, but you'd kind o' miss the Joyce-O'Casey atmosphere.' (Dublin Opinion)*

## A HARD DAY'S HOMEWORK

'Before you went to bed you punched your breakfast programme into your computer. Selecting a tape from your collection, you set it to start playing at 7.45 a.m. You set the coffee maker for the same time, and the toaster for 8.00 a.m.

After breakfast, it is time to go to work. Unlike the old days, it is not necessary to leave the building. You return to the computer and type in a request for the day's schedule. It is printed on a screen in front of you. Any information you require can be presented in this way. You can read all your correspondence on the screen and compose and send replies through the computer which will send the message to your correspondent's computer.

Money is, of course, obsolete. Virtually everything is organised through your computer, your bank's computer — and into yours for information — by your company's computer.

When it comes to shopping, the system is quite similar. You type a set of orders into a computer and ask it to transmit it to the supermarket's computer. When the order is received, the goods are gathered from stock and sent to your house. The bill is paid by automatic transfer from your account to that of the supermarket, by computer.

For leisure in the evening you have a wide choice of television. At this stage everything that has ever been recorded is available. You punch in a request to see the television guide, and ask for the Humphrey Bogart Films List. You type in the reference number for 'Casablanca' and it is shown in your living room. This is recorded in the same way as a telephone call, and you are charged a small fee which is divided between the TV cable company and the film makers.

The children have been playing video games in their room. They brought them to the screen in the same way, through typing in a request.

The appartment hums with satisfaction as you put the cat out and turn to get the tapes for tomorrow. Then the power fails . . . *Dermot Stokes*

### ACKNOWLEDGEMENTS

We list the many people and organisations who have given permission to reproduce illustrations and we acknowledge and thank them. Below we also state the sources for other illustrations. In instances where we have failed to trace the copyright holder we would be grateful if they would contact the publisher.

Bord Fáilte Éireann 2, 22 top, 24 left, 33, 83, 98 top; Columbia-EMI-Warner Distributors Ltd. 126; Frances Breen 73; Cambridge University Collection 19, 21; Dublin Opinion (Frank Kelly) 64 bot., 91 bot., 96, 97 top left, 27 top and bottom; Dublin Port & Docks Board 125 top r.; E.S.B. 55, 64 top; George Gmelch 44, 45 bot., 47, 115; Peter Harding 52, 103; Colm Henry 119; Hot Press 93; Irish Army Air Corps 113, 119; *Irish Chronicle* (Holinshed 1577, Dolmen Edition 1979) 30; I.D.A. 109; Illustrated London News 77 (1866) courtesy RTE; Irish Independent 97 bot.; *Irish Pictures* (Lovett 1888) 1, 6, 53 bot.; Irish Press 10, 89; *The Irish Times* 122 (Martin Turner); *The Irish Town* (Shaffrey 1975) 24 r., 25, 27; Thomas Mason 5; Max Factor 92; National Library of Ireland 40, 46, 50, 56, 58 bot., 60, 65, 66, 72, 78 top, 78 bot. by A. Brioscú, 80, 81, 82, 101; National Museum of Ireland 23, 58 top, 71; Northern Ireland Tourist Board 41; *The Observer* 125 bot.; Eamonn O'Dwyer 90, 94, 95, 104, 106, 116, 120; *Pacata Hibernica* (Stafford 1633) 36; Public Records Office Northern Ireland 69; R.T.E. 74, 86, 100 bot.; Shannon Development 88; Adrian Slattery 9, 20, 22 bot., 28, 35, 37, 38 top, 39, 49, 53 top, 59 after drawing in *Wheel & Spindle* McCutcheon Blackstaff Pr., 70 84, 85, 98, 102 based on Dublin Corporation data; John Speed 29; *The Town in Ulster* (Camlin 1951) 26, 34, 38 bot.; *The Town Wall*

*Fortifications of Ireland* (Fleming 1914) 3; *Truths about Whiskey* Dublin 1878 61; U.N.O. 87; Ulster Museum 57; Richard Willson, *The Ecologist* 123.

We would also like to thank and acknowledge the following for permission to reproduce the various literary extracts: Chatto & Windus Ltd. for extract from *Twenty Years A-growing* by Maurice O'Sullivan; Tony Connor for 'Entering the City' from *Lodgers* by Tony Connor; Faber and Faber Ltd. for 'The Unknown Citizen' from Collected Shorter Poems by W. H. Auden; Katherine K. Kavanagh for 'Requiem for a Mild' by Patrick Kavanagh; Dr. Brendan Kennelly for 'Celtic Ireland' a 7-13th century poem translated by Brendan Kennelly; Lawrence Pollinger Ltd. for 'Flat Suburbs, S.W.', in the Morning' by D. H. Lawrence; Little, Brown and Company for 'Southbound on the Freeway' from *New and Selected Things Taking Place* by May Swenson; Northern Songs for 'Eleanor Rigby' by John Lennon and Paul McCartney; The O'Brien Press for extracts from *After the Wake* by Brendan Behan; The Octagon Press Ltd. for 'Memories of a Survivor' by Doris Lessing; Pan Books for extract of ballad 'The Rocky Road to Dublin' from Old Irish Street Ballads; Routledge & Kegan Paul Ltd. for extracts from *The Hard Road to the Klondyke* by Michael McGowan; Rubert Hart-Davis for 'Cynddylan on a Tractor' by R. S. Thomas; The Society of Authors for extract from *Ulysses* by James Joyce; Dermot Stokes for 'An Ear's Eyeful'.

In some cases we have been unable to trace the copyright holders and we would be grateful for information on the copyright ownership for these items.

We would also like to thank the following who supplied valuable information: Confederation of Irish Industry, Dublin Corporation, Dublin Port and Docks Board, Garda Síochána and the National Manpower Agency.